# GETTING INTO

y

CAREERS

c c C 3

TROTMAN

D0307829

*Getting into Physiotherapy*

This second edition published in 2002
by Trotman and Company Ltd
2 The Green, Richmond, Surrey TW9 1PL
First edition published 2000

© Trotman and Company Limited 2002

British Library Cataloguing in Publication Data
A catalogue record for this book is available from the
British Library.

ISBN 0 85660 855 6

Typeset by Mac Style Ltd, Scarborough, N. Yorkshire

Printed and bound in Great Britain
by Creative Print and Design (Wales) Ltd

# CONTENTS

# ABOUT THE AUTHOR

Laurel Alexander is a complementary therapist and career management consultant in health-related careers. She specialises in complementary breast cancer care and the natural treatment of menopausal symptoms.

Laurel has spoken on stress management at Dryad and Seeboard seminars and has facilitated health and life management programmes for both the public and private sectors. She has appeared on Meridian TV giving advice on stress management, and on radio phone-ins giving guidance on natural health and beauty. She writes for magazines such as *Good Health*, *Positive Health*, *Health Advisor*, *Yoga and Health* and other titles. Her other books include *Getting into Complementary Therapies* and *Getting into Healthcare Professions*, also published by Trotman.

# ACKNOWLEDGEMENTS

I would like to extend my thanks to Raquel Simpson and Prabh Salaman of the Chartered Society of Physiotherapy who have helped me gather together much of the information in this book and to all the health professionals who gave of their time for the case studies.

# The Student Book 2003

**24th Edition £14.99**

0 85660 758 4

www.Careers-Portal.co.uk

## Includes:

- ◆ What it's like sections on all the UK's 280 institutions
- ◆ University/college department rankings
- ◆ Advice on all the major issues including drink, drugs and poverty

The frankest and fullest guide to student life

**The Sunday Telegraph**

The straight-talking A-Z of Universities and Colleges

**The Independent**

# INTRODUCTION

Physiotherapy is a science-based medical subject that looks at how the body moves, how muscles, bones, joints and ligaments work and how they react to pain and trauma. Physiotherapists diagnose ailments that affect muscles and nerves and then treat the patient. It is also their job to look for any predisposing factors that may have contributed to the patient's condition and to advise them on how to minimise the risk of the same thing happening again.

Physiotherapists work with many different situations including:

- helping women in relation to pregnancy
- working with AIDS patients
- helping people deal with stress and anxiety
- improving the confidence of those with mental illness through exercise and recreation
- helping children deal with mental and physical disabilities
- caring for the elderly
- developing the potential of those with learning difficulties through exercise, sport and recreation
- helping sportspeople recover from injury
- teaching people the best way to move and lift in order to prevent or slow the onset of problems such as RSI
- working with the terminally ill or those in intensive care
- helping orthopaedic patients after spinal operations or joint replacements and treating those debilitated following an accident.

Physiotherapists can work in the National Health Service (NHS), where they are the fourth largest profession after doctors, nurses and midwives, in private practice or industry. All of the above are what are called 'clinical' roles, but physiotherapists may also work in research, management or teaching. One thing that is required for all physiotherapy careers, however, is the completion of a three- or four-year degree course. With there being so much demand for places on physiotherapy degree courses there is obviously plenty of competition. But this book

1

will help you work through the various stages towards becoming a fully qualified physiotherapist.

As well as qualified physiotherapists, there are also physiotherapy assistants, who often form an important part of the team. You do not need to have a degree to be an assistant, although there are other qualifications, such as National Vocational Qualifications (NVQs), which are important in helping assistants to develop their learning and their roles. Some physiotherapy assistants are very content with their supporting role and make that their career; others use it as a step towards fully qualified status. There are now courses that are specially dedicated in helping assistants to gain the required qualifications to make the move towards being a physiotherapist.

To work in the NHS all physiotherapists must be what are called 'state registered' and most physiotherapists are 'chartered'. These two terms will be explained in more depth later in the book in Chapter 17.

To help you to decide whether physiotherapy is the career for you, this book will look at the areas in which you can develop your career, whether working in a hospital or in the community, in industry or in the private sector. It discusses academic careers as a physiotherapist and explores the opportunities for working overseas. It also discusses ways of returning to physiotherapy after a break and the role of physiotherapy assistants. Finally, it considers the role of the professional bodies.

## PERSONAL QUALITIES

Physiotherapists are often in a situation where they are working through a course of treatment with a patient, sometimes needing to coax him or her to do something that is not particularly pleasant. Even if this isn't the case, most physiotherapists are in close contact with people and so need to:

■ have good interpersonal skills
■ be caring
■ demonstrate sensitivity
■ be firm when the situation requires it.

Because of the physical nature of the job physiotherapists quite often tend to be sporty, but even if sport is not your favourite pastime you will be expected to be:

- fit
- active
- healthy.

# Chapter 1
# DEVELOPING YOUR CAREER IN PHYSIOTHERAPY

A physiotherapist has a huge choice of areas in which to work. The first opportunity for physiotherapy students to see which area they might like to work in, once they have qualified, is during the 1000 hours of clinical placements they are required to complete in order to qualify for their degree. A clinical placement means the students work alongside fully qualified physiotherapists in a clinical setting, usually in the NHS but sometimes in private practice, to experience interaction with patients and to test their learning to date under strict supervision.

On completion of the degree, the next opportunity to test different areas of practice in physiotherapy is the minimum of two years in which they undertake rotations in the National Health Service. This is usually the stage at which graduates settle on their chosen specialism, if they are planning to specialise. However, it's important to remember that not all physiotherapists do.

Once qualified, all physiotherapists are expected to support their practice with continued professional development (CPD). And if a physio wants to work in a specialist area, such as animal physiotherapy, or to use acupuncture, he or she will have to undertake further study before being allowed to practise in these areas.

The Chartered Society of Physiotherapy (CSP), which is the UK's professional, educational and trade union body, has many recognised clinical interest and occupational groups (CIGs) representing the diversity of the profession (for details of how to contact the different clinical interest groups turn to the back of the book). CIGs are another way of learning more about a particular specialism as they bring together physiotherapists from all over the UK to discuss, share and develop knowledge and clinical practice in their particular area of interest. Physiotherapy students can be members of some CIGs, many of which produce their own newsletters or journals, helping members keep up to

date with what's going on. The list of CIGs gives some idea of the breadth of roles that physiotherapists play. It is worth noting here that some physios prefer to stay generalists, and there are plenty of areas, such as working in the community, that call for a generalist approach.

Whichever area physios end up practising in, there is one thing that is common – a whole-person approach. Physios are trained to look beyond the patient's immediate condition and to take on board other elements that may be pertinent, such as the person's state of mind and what other stresses they may be experiencing.

The rest of this chapter highlights just some of the many different areas open to physiotherapists.

# WORKING IN SPORTS MEDICINE

Physiotherapy and sports go hand in hand, at least when you realise that behind every sporting team or activity there is almost invariably a physiotherapist at work. Physiotherapists specialising in sports medicine need good musculoskeletal skills as these form the majority of treatments they need to administer. They will often be dealing with soft tissue injuries, strains and sprains. But they also have an important rehabilitation role in cases where sports men and women have sustained a more serious injury that perhaps requires surgery, such as a knee operation. Then they will be required to work out an individual programme of exercises and rehab treatment to get the player back to form as quickly as possible. The exact nature of treatment varies with the type of sportsperson the physiotherapist is treating – a rower, for example, will present with quite different problems from a basketball player.

Practitioners in this field may often be working with other medical colleagues as part of the medical team, in which case decisions may be jointly made, or made by the doctor. Often though, it is solely down to the physiotherapist's judgement whether or not a player should be returning to the field.

Opportunities for physios exist in a huge range of sports, from football and rugby to marathon running, basketball and even underwater hockey!

Physios have won places to travel round the world with British teams in the Olympics, Commonwealth Games, football World Cup and many others. But while some of these physios are well-paid employees of their clubs, many will be working in a voluntary capacity and may even have to raise funds to pay for the trip themselves.

**CASE STUDY**

Lynda qualified as a chartered physiotherapist in 1975 and her first job was at the Nottingham City Hospital. She became a senior physiotherapist in charge of the outpatient physiotherapy department and hydrotherapy pool in 1978 but then in 1981 left the NHS to meet the challenge of setting up a private practice. The business grew over the years until by 1995 she was director and owner of three physiotherapy clinics in the Nottinghamshire and Derbyshire areas, and employed nine staff. Working in private practice increased her exposure to sport and sports injuries and so what had started out as a casual involvement with a few local athletes rapidly expanded so that by 1990, she was appointed physiotherapist to the England women's hockey U21 squad. Private practice allowed her the flexibility that was necessary to increase her involvement with sports teams and in 1994 Lynda moved on from hockey to become Governing Body Physiotherapist for the national weightlifting squad. During the past ten years Lynda has worked with many different sports and at a variety of training camps and competitions but has worked most extensively with tennis and has enjoyed the challenge of treating both able-bodied and wheelchair players. Three years ago she decided to sell the clinics to allow herself more time to work and travel with elite sports squads and Lynda now works as a freelance sports physiotherapist and is currently developing the role of Sports Medicine Manager at Loughborough University.

'The highlights of my sporting career have most definitely been my attendances at the Atlanta and Sydney Olympic Games, the past two Commonwealth Games and seven World University Games. Although working at a major sporting event is often extremely demanding, both physically and emotionally, being there and sharing in the successes and disappointments of other team members is a most remarkable experience. I am therefore delighted to have been appointed Chief Physiotherapist for Team England for the Commonwealth Games in Manchester 2002.'

Of course sports physios don't always have such a high profile as Lynda in this case study. Many work in private practice, for sports and leisure clubs or for local teams, and play a key role in keeping amateur sportspeople on their feet.

# WORKING WITH THE ELDERLY

By the year 2026 it is predicted that 13 million people of retirement age will be living in Britain. Not only is Britain's population ageing, but also with lifestyle changes and medical breakthroughs people are living longer. The view of many analysts is that the ageing population will put pressure on the health service and that more professionals will be needed with particular expertise in caring for the elderly. Physiotherapists play a very important role in treating and rehabilitating elderly patients. Falling is a serious problem for the elderly – 2000 deaths occur every year as a result of a fall at home – and many physios are directly involved in working to reduce elderly people's falls. Helping to improve their mobility and balance, by designing exercise programmes for them, is just one of the things that physios are doing to help counter this problem. Of course, elderly care physios do not just deal with problems such as falling; they will be helping patients with a multitude of conditions such as Parkinson's disease and dementia. Working in this field is likely to become more and more interesting as the emphasis on the need to care for our elderly population becomes more of a healthcare priority.

# WORKING WITH CHILDREN

Enjoying working with children is clearly one of the main prerequisites for specialising in paediatrics. Jenny, a senior II physiotherapist at one of England's primary children's hospitals, says 'It's vital to put yourself on the children's wavelength to get the best results from working with them. You have to use your imagination and try to make things into a game, if possible. If a child has weak legs, for example, you develop play activities around standing and before they know it they are exercising their legs without even realising it.' Supporting parents and carers is another vital aspect of the role. Jenny stresses the importance of keeping parents fully informed and involving them at every stage of the treatment programme. This is especially relevant because parents are usually the people maintaining the child's treatment at home. Being a good communicator is therefore one of the key requirements of specialising in this field.

Paediatric physios may be working with a whole range of conditions, such as juvenile chronic arthritis, cerebral palsy, cystic fibrosis, dyspraxia and with children with congenital deformities, foot problems and unusual gait (how people walk) patterns. It can also be particularly emotionally stressful working with children who are terminally ill. But those who work in this area say that, while it carries its own challenges, it is deeply rewarding and can be enormous fun.

## WORKING WITH LEARNING DISABILITIES

Non-verbal communication is an important aspect of working in the field of learning disabilities as sometimes patients, or clients as they are often referred to in this area, have limited or no spoken language. Rachael, a specialist physio in this field, says it is 'very different from other areas of physiotherapy, needing high levels of determination, patience and an ability to interpret through body language rather than just relying on words'. But she says that one of the biggest challenges can be coping with other people's attitudes to those with learning disabilities. 'You have to be prepared to act as an advocate on behalf of your clients,' she says. 'People with learning disabilities are often treated differently – people tend to see only the disability.'

Making the physiotherapy treatment fun is also very important, especially as the benefits of the treatment cannot necessarily be explained, as they can with other client groups. Physios working with learning disabilities often use hydrotherapy, gymnastics and rebound therapy (on a trampoline) in their treatment programmes.

Finally, students or newly qualified physios need to demonstrate real patience if they are hoping to specialise in this field. 'Goals in learning disabilities can take months, even years, to achieve so you have to set them small enough and pace yourself – even if it's only the client acknowledging your presence,' explains Rachael. 'You have to rethink traditional strategies and be prepared to wait. Your first result may be small, but it will be worth the wait,' she concludes.

## WORKING WITH ANIMALS

Some physiotherapy graduates prefer to focus on animals rather than people. You can do this by undertaking postgraduate training in animal therapy, but two years of general practice must be completed first before embarking on certificated courses run by the Association of Chartered Physiotherapists in Animal Therapy (ACPAT) (see clinical interest and occupational groups at the back of the book). Once qualified, all chartered animal physiotherapists must continue to attend ACPAT courses in order to keep up their professional development. In addition, physios working with animals can only do so with veterinary approval, so liaison with the Royal College of Veterinary Surgeons is very important.

It is important to gain as much experience in the human field as possible and keeping up to date with both physiotherapy and veterinary techniques and practice is vital. Animal physiotherapists have to use exactly the same skills that physios working with human patients do, albeit in a different setting, and will often need to employ mobilisation, manipulation and electrotherapy skills to treat an animal patient.

Because of the nature of the work, physiotherapists specialising in animal therapy tend to be private practitioners, either running their own practices or working in another set-up. Some also link their work to sport, through, for example, being official chartered physiotherapists in horse jumping, dressage and horse racing.

## CASE STUDY

Charlotte chose physiotherapy as a career after reading a number of newspaper articles about an animal physiotherapist, and qualified in 1993 from Middlesex and University College Hospital aged 21. As with most specialisations, the basic grade had to be completed before any intensive training could be initiated in animal therapy and she spent almost all of her annual leave for two years travelling from Surrey to Yorkshire on work experience with the particular lady about whom the newspaper articles had been written. Charlotte completed her basic grade, then did an 18-month apprenticeship in Yorkshire, and worked for a couple of other animal physios and veterinary surgeons before establishing her own business, physio4animals, in 1997. Her career has developed both in clinical terms and in teaching capacities and she is responsible for the clinical training and qualifying of five student animal physiotherapists and regularly takes short-term clinical placements for MSc students. Between her equine and canine clinical work, students and business, Charlotte pursues her CPD, which often involves travelling to the US, and she enjoys representing Britain alongside the Ridden Endurance teams as their physiotherapist looking after horse and rider (although the horses always come first and the riders are seen if Charlotte has time after stables close and before bed!).

Charlotte says, 'It is a wonderful career to be involved in but there are a lot of down sides too and they should be seriously considered before embarking on the training and a full-time career in animal physiotherapy; extremely long days, cold, dark early mornings, several hours a day in the car, you and your car permanently smelling of horses and dogs, constantly feeling exhausted and you will never be rich. Apart from that it is exhilarating, moving, fun, exciting, interesting and above all utterly satisfying!'

# Chapter 2
# GETTING ON TO A DEGREE PROGRAMME

Before you can choose the area in which you may want to specialise, you need to get qualified!

## ACADEMIC REQUIREMENTS

It has already been mentioned that physiotherapy is one of the most popular degree courses in the UK, so naturally there is strong competition for every available place. Entry requirements are the same as for any degree programme, but the level of demand means that conditional offers of a place will be set higher than the minimum. To obtain a place on any course you will need to demonstrate the ability to study at a high academic level as well as apply your knowledge in a practical manner. A variety of qualifications may be accepted and it is important to check directly with the individual university before you apply.

### England, Wales and Northern Ireland

School leavers are normally required to have three A2-level subjects at a minimum of grade C and above (one should be biological science) and normally four A1 levels at grade B including a biological science. In addition to the above, students should hold a minimum of five GCSEs at grade C and above. The latter should be taken at one sitting and include mathematics, English language and a spread of science subjects. The typical A-level profile of a school leaver accepted for all programmes in 2000 was 24 A-level points (the equivalent of three Bs).

### Scotland

A typical student profile is five SCE Highers at grades AABBB taken at one sitting (minimum of two science subjects).

# Eire

School leavers should have an Irish Leaving Certificate with a minimum of four passes in subjects at higher level – two at B grade and two at C grade.

A range of alternative qualifications equivalent to the above may be accepted, but prospective students are strongly advised to contact the institutions to which they intend to apply for their specific requirements. Examples of alternative qualifications are:

- BTEC (Edexcel)/HND National Diploma in Health Studies (science) with distinctions/merits in all units
- GNVQ in Health and Social Care/Science (most institutions require a biological science A2-level in addition to these)
- NVQ Level III in appropriate topic plus A2-level biology at least grade C or above
- International Baccalaureate
- Certain Access courses (individual institutions should be asked which Access courses they recognise for entry to their physiotherapy programme)
- Open University foundation course in science
- Degree: normally a 2:1 honours degree in a related academic discipline.

# Mature students

Physiotherapy is a profession open to the older student. At present approximately 34 per cent of all UK physiotherapy students are over 21 when they begin training. Before you can be accepted on to a physiotherapy programme you will need to show evidence of successful recent academic study, which should be science related.

If you have no qualifications beyond GCSE level then it will be necessary for you to obtain some form of qualification. Please refer to the list of alternative qualifications above. If you already hold a degree you will not necessarily have immediate access to physiotherapy. If it is several years since you completed your degree, particularly if it was in an arts subject, then it may be advisable for you to study biology or human biology A-level.

## Work experience

You will need to gain work experience and show evidence that you have worked with people in the community (preferably within the NHS) if you are to be offered a place. Work-shadowing physiotherapists in specialist areas such as private practice or sports clinics is generally not enough. You could apply for an unpaid volunteer position on a part-time basis or you might try to shadow a physiotherapist for a day or two and supplement this with a volunteer job in another caring environment such as a hospice, old people's home or in the children's ward of your local hospital. You need to demonstrate your commitment by doing something on a regular basis throughout the year or for at least two weeks in a hospital position. To find work experience approach local hospitals with physiotherapy departments or look in the phone book under physiotherapy clinics. You could look on the Internet on the site www.therapy-world.co.uk/physio.htm for lists of physiotherapists. Write a letter to the physiotherapy department or clinic, including the name of a referee, someone who can vouch for your interest in physiotherapy as well as your reliability.

When you are actually in your work placement, ask the physiotherapist for the technical names of the procedures you see and for information on the techniques and equipment used. Ask about the advantages and disadvantages of different types of treatments, and in what situations they are used. Ask the physiotherapist about his or her life, the hours, the salary, the demands of the job and career options.

## Further considerations

Several things must be carefully considered when deciding whether the time is right for you to return to study. Admissions tutor Sara says: 'The majority of physiotherapy programmes are full time, lasting for either three or four years. This has obvious financial implications for someone who is used to earning a salary and people need to be realistic about whether they can support themselves financially throughout this time.' Another important point to remember when considering physiotherapy as a career change is that it may involve lengthy clinical placements outside your hometown. This can present difficulties for mature students who are more likely to own their own home or have partners and children. Despite this, many older people successfully complete their degrees in physiotherapy every year, and go on to have long and successful careers. Sara says: 'The mature students who do make the commitment often turn out to be some of our best students, despite having to juggle a hectic lifestyle. They are aware they are making sacrifices to be at university so are determined to get the best out of it.'

As well as having the ability to cope with the academic demands of an honours degree course in science, admissions tutors will also be looking for evidence of the following qualities and skills in potential students:

- communication, helping and caring skills
- sensitivity and tolerance
- ability to use initiative
- potential to undertake an intensive course of study
- reliability, honesty and trustworthiness
- enthusiasm, dedication and determination.

**CASE STUDY**

Maeve, now in her thirties, decided she wished to become a physiotherapist when her children reached school age. Her first step was to enrol on an A-level course in human biology, which she completed in a year, gaining a grade A. She said: 'Having been outside the education system for so long, even going back to college to study an A-level was quite daunting, but the feeling of elation when I passed and was accepted on to a physiotherapy degree course was worth every minute of the studying. I'm now in my final year and I won't say it has been easy to find the time to study, or to take the drop in income, but finally I feel I will be doing something satisfying in my work. At times it's felt like a bit of a long hard slog, but I don't regret a single minute of it.'

# OTHER REQUIREMENTS

The personal statement and references are important parts of the University and Colleges Admissions Service (UCAS) application and these will be read very carefully. Admissions tutor John said: 'We need to know just why candidates want to study physiotherapy and exactly what they think it is. It is very useful if candidates have visited physiotherapy departments prior to making their application. This gives them a broader understanding of the profession and allows them to demonstrate more clearly why they think it is one which they would be good at and enjoy. We also look for someone who has shown a commitment to physiotherapy by doing some voluntary work or work experience and like them to be able to tell us just what they learnt from that. Someone's interests are also very revealing – things that they have been involved in at school or in the community. Physiotherapy obviously involves working closely with other people – both patients and colleagues – and it is important that applicants can show an ability to work well with others.'

# CRIMINAL RECORDS

Because chartered physiotherapists work in a position of trust, often on a one-to-one basis with children and vulnerable adults, you must disclose any criminal record that you may have. Some criminal convictions will prevent you from gaining state registration to practise as a physiotherapist. It would be advisable to discuss any criminal conviction with the course admissions tutor at the university of your choice, before applying for a course.

# HEALTH SCREENING

As physiotherapy is an extremely physically and emotionally demanding profession, it is important that students are physically and mentally fit before starting a course, and health assessments are compulsory. You will usually be asked to complete a health questionnaire on being offered a place, and confirmation of a place will be conditional on you being considered fit enough to deal with the course.

# EQUAL OPPORTUNITIES

Both the Chartered Society of Physiotherapy and the institutions offering its approved degree programmes are working to widen access to their programmes and welcome applications from individuals regardless of gender, age, race, ethnic origin, sexual orientation or religion.

If you have a physical disability or serious injury you will be offered an assessment of the disability to ensure you are able to meet the physical demands of the course and the profession. The admissions tutor will be able to advise you on this. Applicants with a visual impairment are offered support by the Royal National Institute for the Blind (RNIB) to train on mainstream physiotherapy programmes. Students are advised to discuss their application with the RNIB, which will be able to advise on the type of support it is able to offer. Further information is available from the RNIB, 105 Judd Street, London WC1H 9NE. Tel: 020 7388 1266. Website: www.rnib.org.uk.

# SCHOOLS OF PHYSIOTHERAPY

More than 30 universities in England and Wales, Scotland and Ireland now offer a BSc in physiotherapy. Most require you to submit your application through UCAS and you are allowed to apply for six courses in total. A list of institutions offering physiotherapy programmes is given at the back of the book.

It is worth spending some time thinking about all the things that will be important to you during the years you spend studying. As well as the physiotherapy programme itself, you should consider whether you would be happiest based in a large city or a smaller town, the size of university you would like to attend, the surrounding hospitals in which you will be undertaking your clinical placements, the types of facilities offered by the university and opportunities for involvement in extracurricular activities such as sports teams, etc.

It is advisable to ensure your entry reaches UCAS between 1 September and 15 December for entry the following autumn. Late applications can be processed, but your chances of being considered will be greatly reduced, as programmes are unlikely to have vacancies.

# Chapter 3
# COURSE STRUCTURE

A typical course is divided into blocks of study and clinical placements, with the amount of time spent on clinical placements increasing each year. The curriculum is based on the notion that the learning achieved by students in university and on clinical placement is of equal value and should be totally integrated.

Often students will share modules with students of occupational therapy, radiography or nursing – for example anatomy, psychology and professional studies. However, there will also be classes that are purely for physiotherapists, such as human movement and therapeutic exercise, electrotherapy and manual therapy.

The amount of contact hours is very high – usually comparable to the time spent in a full-time job – and a variety of teaching methods is used, including lectures, tutorials, seminars and practical workshops. All courses focus on rigorous clinical education that provides broad experience in the management and treatment of patients with a wide variety of problems and disorders.

Assessment will include a combination of academic coursework (essays, laboratory reports and presentations), written and practical exams, clinical assessments and research work.

Many lecturers are lecturer/practitioners, meaning that they continue to work as clinicians as well as teach. Course leader Gillian said: 'The courses are very intensive and students need to absorb a lot of knowledge and be able to translate this into physiotherapy practice. Alongside practical skills such as therapeutic exercise, manual therapy and electrophysical techniques, we also help student physiotherapists to develop good communication skills – written, verbal and non-verbal – as well as time, people and self-management skills. They need to learn to assess individuals, taking into account physical, social, psychological and cultural needs, and to plan effective treatments. They are also given practical experience in research and evaluation, which enables them to evaluate critically published research and apply the findings as appropriate, as well as going on to pursue their own research projects.'

Physiotherapists need to understand their patients and their work in the context of the environment that surrounds them, and students also learn about the organisations they may work in, for example acute hospital trusts, health centres, GP surgeries, hospices, industry, schools and patients' homes, as well as legal, ethical and professional issues.

A large part of a physiotherapist's work focuses on promoting healthier living and preventive techniques and this is also an important area of study.

**CASE STUDY**

Lucy is in the final year of her degree programme and has undertaken placements in various hospitals, social service departments and day centres while studying. She said: 'Clinical placements are so important. They allow you to put into practice all the theory, which you absorb in the classroom, and to take back your experiences with you to apply in the classroom situation. Although you have constant supervision when you're on placement, at the end of the day you are working with real patients and you can see the results of your treatments. It also teaches you a lot about yourself and the areas of work that appeal to you. When I enrolled on my course I thought that I would like to work with children, but after undertaking a clinical placement in a hospital I know that I want to work with the elderly. There is no better way of learning and it reinforces all the academic study you do in university as well as giving you new knowledge and skills.'

## Course structure

The first year covers the study of the theory and practical issues underlying physiotherapy including:

- anatomy
- physiology
- kinesiology (the study of the mechanics of body movement)
- research methods
- musculoskeletal conditions
- cardiovascular and respiratory functions
- communication and clinical skills.

The second year divides the time between academic study and clinical placements in settings such as hospital wards, physiotherapy outpatient departments and specialised units within hospitals and the community. Students are expected to spend at least 1000 hours on clinical placements, and will typically experience a wide range of areas, such as orthopaedics, neurology, outpatients, care of the elderly, medical and general surgical wards and respiratory and cardiovascular units, including intensive care. They may also have the opportunity to work in learning disability, mental illness, obstetrics, paediatrics, burns, spinal injuries and in the community. Areas covered include:

- neurology
- clinical education
- pathophysiology
- clinical placements.

The third year is also split between clinical and academic study. Areas covered include:

- pain management
- exercise science
- neurorehabilitation
- option topics such as sports science, burns and plastic surgery, mental health
- clinical placements (students usually spend about 20 weeks of the course on clinical placements).

## CASE STUDY

Susan is a lecturer in physiotherapy and one of her responsibilities is to arrange clinical placements for 70 students each year. She said: 'It is important that students undertake a variety of placements so that they cover the key areas such as neuro, respiratory, outpatients, orthopaedics and care of the elderly. We also want them to experience as wide a range of settings as possible, so they may go to a teaching hospital, a community setting and to a district general hospital, for example. They obviously become more competent and get more involved as the course progresses, so while they might be seeing upper and lower limb conditions in a second year outpatient placement, in the third year we would expect them to be seeing spinal conditions. The main aim is for undergraduates to develop clinical reasoning for assessment and problem solving. That is something which we cannot teach in college. The development of personal skills – communicating with colleagues, patients and their relatives – is also very important, as is learning to manage their own workload.'

# Chapter 4
# STUDENT ELECTIVES

Many students undertake an elective or study visit overseas, often during the summer break, between their penultimate and final year at university. Before you decide to head off it is important to consider what you want to gain from the experience and how you think it will fit into your overall career plan.

Another important consideration is language. How will you communicate with your patients? Do you speak any foreign languages or will you be reliant on someone to interpret for you? Are your personal skills enough for you to get by alone, often working in a very different environment to the ones you are used to, and within a culture which is not your own?

To many people these factors are part of the excitement and the challenge, and many students say they return much stronger and with more innovation as a result of their overseas experience. However, it is important to consider whether you are one of these people, or whether you might gain experience just as valuable from undertaking an elective in the UK.

## CASE STUDY

Tamsin and Nicola undertook an elective of three weeks in Sri Lanka, where they were assigned one interpreter between the two of them. Nicola said: 'We used the interpreter whenever possible, but we soon found that our non-verbal communication skills improved greatly! Our largest client group was ex-soldiers, many of whom had been injured by landmines following the civil war. We were assessing patients before, during and after the limb-making process and gave advice and information about stump care as well as teaching people how to use their new limbs. The cultural differences were very much in evidence. For example, most patients slept on the floor and had a squat toilet at home and a lot of them were farmers, spending around ten hours a day working in fields, so they needed to be very agile with their new limbs.' The two also became involved in a community rehabilitation project that presented many challenges, not least driving around in a jeep for 12 hours a day to visit just a handful of patients in rural areas. With some properties inaccessible by vehicle, the drive would often be followed by a short trek through the jungle. Nicola said: 'The isolation in which people lived, coupled with their Buddhist beliefs that disabilities have occurred as a result of actions in a previous life, often meant that patients were reluctant to try to improve their situation. However, one of the aspects of Sri Lanka that I will always remember was the warmth of the people, their resourcefulness and their eagerness to learn. We also gained a deep understanding of the importance of listening to a patient's personal beliefs in order to truly address their needs.'

**CASE STUDY**

Immediately after completing his exams in the UK, newly qualified physiotherapist James found a placement with a charity that arranged for him to travel to a small town in the eastern highlands of Zimbabwe. His first impression of the government-funded hospital was of severe poverty – even basic equipment was in short supply, with drips hanging from window pegs and thin mattresses on simple metal frames, which were not adjustable in height, packed closely together. James said: 'The essentials were all there, but in very small numbers. There was a two-bed intensive care unit, four medical wards, an orthopaedic/surgical ward, an obstetric ward, and small paediatric unit and outpatient clinics. I worked alongside a physiotherapy team of four, and being part of such a small team meant that I gained experience in a wide range of areas. Because the numbers were so low, no speciality services had developed.' James worked with many patients with burns – open fires used for cooking and heating meant burns were common in winter months – and also people with AIDS-related neuropathies. The local timber industry also meant that men who had chronic back problems from using poor lifting techniques populated outpatient clinics.

James said: 'Physiotherapy treatment was primarily functional, including pressure relief, traction for fractures, as the hospital didn't have the funds or experience to fixate internally, and teaching wheelchair skills. One difficulty I encountered was treating children with cerebral palsy. Many of them were very scared of Caucasians and would scream when I tried to approach them. It made treatment almost impossible and the only alternative was to try to use non-verbal communication to show their mothers how to take part in their child's treatment and to continue it at home. The greatest frustration I encountered was not the limited resources, but the added complications that I encountered, such as pressure sores or permanent deformity from malaligned fractures. However, any difficulties I came across were worth it to me for the personal development from the huge range of conditions that I saw and helped to treat, and for the range of skills I gained.'

# FUNDING

Funding is an important consideration when planning an elective overseas – the last thing you want is to find yourself unhappy and with no money in a strange country. In addition to the cost of getting there you will also need to calculate how much money you will need for living expenses, accommodation and travel. Some departments also charge an administrative fee for accepting an overseas student.

One source of funding is the Joe Jeans Memorial Fund, jointly funded by the CSP's Charitable Trust and Forester Health. The fund was set up five years ago and aims to help people with the costs of a placement that will enable them to develop their clinical experience in a particular specialism, or to gain experience that could not be found in the UK. Further information on this is available from the CSP's Education Department. The department also produces several fact sheets on overseas electives, including information on insurance and visas, sources of funding, ERASMUS (see Chapter 5) and opportunities in individual countries. Contact the students' officer via their website www.csp.org.uk or telephone 020 7306 6666.

The following agencies, while not actually offering funding, may be able to recommend sources of possible funding for a study visit or elective:

- World Health Organization, 1211 Geneva 27, Geneva, Switzerland.
- Student Adviser, Educational Grants Advisory Service, Family Welfare Association, 501–505 Kingsland Road, London E8 4AU.
- British Council, 10 Spring Gardens, London SW1A 2BN.

# Chapter 5
# FUNDING FOR PHYSIOTHERAPY UNDERGRADUATES

Unlike many other students, the majority of physiotherapy students on undergraduate courses have their tuition fees paid for them by the Department of Health. This is because most places in England and Wales are funded under the National Health Service bursaries arrangement.

The NHS provides bursaries for pre-registration physiotherapy programmes for students living and studying in the UK and these are assessed by the Department of Health on behalf of the health authorities under which the degree programme falls.

Physio students in Scotland and Northern Ireland will also have their fees paid, but the funding for this comes from their respective education departments rather than the health departments. This means that arrangements for accessing this funding work in a slightly different way.

## ELIGIBILITY FOR NHS BURSARIES

To be eligible for an NHS bursary you must meet a residence requirement. This usually means you must have been 'ordinarily resident' in the British Isles for the three years before the physiotherapy programme begins. If you were absent for a period only because you or your family were temporarily employed overseas, you will probably be treated as if your residence was uninterrupted. However, if you were only resident in the British Isles to receive full-time education, and you would normally have lived elsewhere, you will not usually be regarded as having been 'ordinarily resident' in the British Isles.

### Means testing

The bursaries for physiotherapy are means tested, which means that your income, or that of your parents or partner, will be taken into account.

Contributions by parents or partners are calculated on the level of their residual income, following tax-deductible allowances. Means-tested bursaries are designed to cover day-to-day living costs so rates vary, for example they are higher in London to reflect the increased cost of living in the capital.

For more information about financial assistance contact the institution to which you have applied. You can also find detailed information about the NHS bursary scheme in the leaflet 'Financial Help for Health Care Students', available from Department of Health, PO Box 777, London SE1 6XH. Email: doh@prologistics.co.uk. Tel (for NHS employees or those working in healthcare): 0541 555455.

Or enquires may be directed as follows:

**England** The NHS Student Grants Unit, 22 Plymouth Road, Blackpool FY3 7JS. Tel: 01253 655655.

**Northern Ireland** The Department of Higher and Further Education Training and Employment, Student Support Branch, 4th Floor, Adelaide House, 39–49 Adelaide Street, Belfast BT2 8FD. Tel: 028 9025 7777.

**Scotland** The Student Awards Agency for Scotland, Gyleview House, 3 Redheughs Rigg, South Gyle, Edinburgh EH12 9HH. Tel: 0131 476 8212.

**Wales** The NHS (Wales) Student Awards Unit, Human Resources Division, The National Assembly for Wales, Cathays Park, Cardiff CF10 3NQ. Tel: 029 2082 6886.

# STUDENT LOANS

The NHS bursary is not intended to cover all of a student's expenses, which means that the remainder has to be met through a student loan. These were introduced as part of the Education (Student Loan) Act 1990 and are administered by the Student Loans Company Ltd. These loans are not means-tested and applications for a loan can normally be made at any time during the academic year, as long as the university certifies that you are eligible.

Students are not asked to start repaying loans until the April after they finish or leave their physiotherapy programme, although individuals may make repayments earlier if they wish. The amount of the loan outstanding is linked to inflation and will track changes in inflation. The outstanding amount is adjusted each year. Repayments may be deferred for a year at a time if your income is low, but you have to prove to the Student Loans Company Ltd that your income is less than 85 per cent of the national average earnings. If payments are deferred the outstanding loan will still increase in line with inflation. For further information about student loans contact: The Student Loans Company Ltd. Tel: 0800 405010. Minicom: 0800 085 3950. Website: www.slc.co.uk.

# OTHER ALLOWANCES

Physiotherapy students may be able to access allowances other than the NHS bursary. These may include:

**Extra weeks attendance** – this reflects the fact that most health professional students have longer academic years than other students. You can get an allowance for each extra week above a set limit of weeks in the year that you are expected to attend. Your course leader will have details of this.

**Excess travel expenses** – this allowance reflects the fact that attending clinical placements, which may be situated some distance away, is an essential part of your training and is payable over and above your normal daily travelling costs.

**Disabled students' allowance** – this is intended to cover the extra costs you incur as a result of disability while training. It is not intended to pay the disability-related costs you would normally have incurred. There are four elements to cover different areas of need:

- the non-medical helper's allowance, to help you pay for sign language interpreters or notetakers
- the specialist equipment allowance, for major items of specialist equipment such as a computer
- the travel allowance, for travel costs reasonably and necessarily incurred due to your disability
- the other costs allowance, to cover any costs related to your disability and study, such as Braille paper or books and tapes, not covered by other allowances.

# UNIFORMS

NHS Executive guidance states that no NHS-funded health professional student should have to pay for their own uniforms. Students are expected to wear uniforms on clinical placements and there may be other occasions when they want to wear them. The guidance was set out in Health Service Circular 1999/072 'Non-medical education and training (NMET) good contracting guidelines'. It states: 'Health professional students should not expect to pay for their uniforms. Consortia must therefore ensure that either the local NHS trust provides the uniforms free of charge or that their cost is specifically included in the contracts negotiated with the HE institutions.'

# PREVIOUS FUNDING

If a student is accepted by a course to fill one of its NHS bursary places then the student will receive that bursary, regardless of any local education authority (LEA) mandatory award previously made. However, students who are not accepted on to one of the bursary places, and who have to apply to their LEA for funding, are unlikely to receive a second mandatory award if they have already had one for a previous course of study. Students who fall into this category should contact their local LEA to discuss eligibility. Mature students are often in this predicament, but it is still possible to receive a further award for the physiotherapy degree.

# WHO ELSE CAN PROVIDE FINANCIAL ASSISTANCE?

## Access loans

If, having taken up your full entitlement to an NHS bursary and loan, you are still in financial difficulty, you can apply to your college or to your students' union for information about Access funds or hardship loans. A detailed application has to be completed and will not be considered unless accompanied by three monthly bank statements.

## Members' Benevolent Fund (MBF)

Provided they are members of the Chartered Society of Physiotherapy, physiotherapy students can now apply for financial assistance from the Society's MBF. This is a recent development as the fund has traditionally existed to support retired members of the profession. However, students have made more applications in recent times and so the Trustees have altered the rules to allow student applications. The Trustees consider each application on a case-by-case basis, but they cannot pay off loans and/or give students funding for books, for example, because these are things meant to be covered by their NHS bursary. Further information is available from: Christine Cox, Members' Benevolent Fund, Chartered Society of Physiotherapy, 14 Bedford Row, London WC1R 4ED. Tel: 020 7306 6666. Website: www.csp.org.uk.

## SOCRATES–ERASMUS

If your physiotherapy programme features cooperation with other European universities approved by the European Commission under SOCRATES–ERASMUS, you may be eligible for a top-up grant towards the cost of studying elsewhere in the EU for between three months and one year. Your course leader may be able to give you additional information about eligibility. For general information about the SOCRATES–ERASMUS scheme, contact: The UK SOCRATES–ERASMUS Council, The Research and Development Building, The University, Canterbury, Kent CT2 7PD. Tel: 01227 762712. Email: erasmus@ukc.ac.uk. Website: www.erasmus.ac.uk.

## The Educational Grants Advisory Service (EGAS)

This is an independent advice agency for people wanting to get funding for further or higher education. It is mainly concerned with helping students not eligible for statutory funding. Those who have received statutory funding but are in extreme financial difficulty despite having explored Access funds, student loans, etc, may be eligible for help. Further information is available from: The Educational Grants Advisory Service (EGAS), The Family Welfare Association, 501–505 Kingsland Road, Dalston, London E8 4AU. Tel: 020 7249 6636.

## Government agencies

The Department for Education and Skills (DfES) has several publications about financial support for students. Contact them at the address below for further details:

- The Department for Education and Skills, DfES Publications, PO Box 5050, Sherwood Park, Annesley, Nottingham NG15 0DJ. Tel: 08700 012345. Website: www.dfes.gov.uk/index.htm.
- For copies of Scotland and Northern Ireland's guides to grants, fees and loans, contact the following:

  - Student Awards Agency for Scotland, Gyleview House, 3 Redheughs Rigg, South Gyle, Edinburgh EH12 9HH. Tel: 0131 476 8212. Website: www.student-support-saas.gov.uk.
  - Department of Education for Northern Ireland, Rathgael House, Balloo Road, Bangor, Co. Down BT19 7PR. Tel: 028 9127 0591. Fax: 028 9146 2744.

A publication worth looking out for is the *Directory of Grant Making Trusts*, published by the Directory of Social Change. As the approximate price for all three volumes is £90 it is advisable to go to your local library and ask whether they keep it in the reference section. (ISBN 1 900 360 829.) Alternatively, call 020 7209 5151 for further information.

# Chapter 6
# LOOKING FOR WORK

So you've qualified and now you are looking for a job. Where do you start?

## Job fairs

If you are on the first rung of your career your university may well be able to help. Some universities organise job fairs, by inviting local trusts to an event, allowing them to advertise their vacancies and sell the benefits of working at that particular trust. One such example is the jobs fair organised by the University of Nottingham for students from five neighbouring universities, which brought together over a dozen trusts.

## Magazines

The main source for job vacancies is in the Chartered Society of Physiotherapy's fortnightly magazine, *Frontline*. This carries a large number of recruitment advertisements in every issue and is split into different classifications to help jobseekers find what they want, including rotational posts. As well as positions in the NHS, *Frontline* carries advertisements from private practitioners wanting staff for their clinics and ads from people wanting to sell their business to a new owner. There is also a section at the back of each magazine with details of locum agencies for the UK and overseas. Jobs Online is the CSP's online jobsearch facility at www.csp.org.uk/jobs.cfm.

Another publication, *Therapy Weekly*, advertises some physiotherapy vacancies, along with jobs for occupational and speech and language therapists. As its name suggests, it is published every week and is distributed directly to hospital departments. It too has a website: www.therapy.co.uk.

# Websites

The following sites specialise in physiotherapy vacancies:

**JW Recruitment Medical Ltd**  www.jwmedical.co.uk/physio.htm

**EM Recruitment**  www.emrecruitment.co.uk/physio.asp

**UK Therapist**  www.uktherapist.co.uk

**Therapy Workline**  www.therapy-workline.co.uk

**Countrywide Medical Selection**  www.countrywidemedical.co.uk

**PhyiosOnline.com**  www.physiosonline.com.

As the Internet becomes more widely used in the health service more trusts are likely to advertise vacancies on their own intranet or website. If you are interested in working in a particular part of the country it may be worth sending off some speculative letters enquiring about vacancies, as physiotherapists tend to be quite a mobile workforce.

# Chapter 7
# STARTING WORK

Newly qualified physiotherapists need to spend approximately two years developing their clinical skills, consolidating the knowledge they have gained at university, acquiring new knowledge through basic research and beginning to take on the role of a teacher, both to patients and to other staff.

## ROTATIONS

The best way of developing clinical skills and knowledge is to become involved in a rotation scheme, in which you work in a range of specialist areas for around three or four months each. Specialisms typically include general medicine and surgery, orthopaedics, neurology, rheumatology, care of elderly people and outpatient work. Many districts will also be able to offer wider experience, which could include paediatrics, intensive care, neurosurgery, cardiothoracic surgery, learning difficulties and mental health.

### Supervision

When planning to join a rotation scheme physiotherapists should look for a supportive and encouraging environment, where senior staff are able to offer adequate supervision. You should have easy access to an experienced physiotherapist who will act as your mentor.

No physiotherapist should practise beyond their scope and new entrants need to recognise the limits of their competency. Advice and assistance from a senior colleague should always be sought if you are not sure of something. Senior managers need to ensure the needs of their service are met, so they will be looking for junior physiotherapists to play a full role in providing that service as soon as possible. However, this will be balanced with the need for new entrants to consolidate, extend and develop their knowledge and skills.

The first two years of practice are crucial in developing an increased understanding of the healthcare environment, gaining confidence in your personal capabilities and role, learning to work with physiotherapy colleagues and professionals in other disciplines such as nurses, doctors, occupational therapists, physiotherapy assistants and porters, and developing clinical reasoning and research skills.

A staff appraisal/individual performance review scheme should be put in place for each new entrant to the profession. This should record personal and professional development and encompass objectives set by the staff physiotherapist and the manager at the beginning of each rotation. These should be evaluated both in the middle and at the end of the rotation and will form part of your continuing professional development programme.

# CONTINUING PROFESSIONAL DEVELOPMENT

Providing a high-quality healthcare service requires well-trained and motivated staff. All members of staff are required to take responsibility for continuously updating and increasing their skills and knowledge by undertaking continuing professional development (CPD) throughout their careers. Failure to do so can be considered to constitute negligence.

The integration of CPD into a physiotherapist's career benefits the patient, the employer and the therapist. CPD covers a range of learning opportunities, both formal and informal. Formal opportunities include undertaking post-qualification courses, attendance at conferences and seminars, and undertaking research and presentation of research papers. Informal CPD ranges from attending in-house training programmes to reading journals and research papers, attending professional body meetings, undertaking secondments and having contact with other professionals.

During the first two years of a rotation programme CPD should include structured as well as informal education programmes, specific to each rotation. This should include time to reflect on practice, teaching sessions, group discussion, analysis of journal articles, presentation of case studies, individual supervision and feedback as well as access to suitable library facilities. Clear objectives relating to these areas, including opportunities as well as duties, should be written down and available to all new entrants.

# Chapter 8
# WHAT KIND OF SALARY CAN YOU EXPECT?

## WITHIN THE NHS

If you are thinking of practising in the NHS you will want to know what kind of salary you can expect to earn. Salaries are dependent on what grade you are on. There are eight scales, although some are rarely used. The government sets pay on these different grades nationally, but other terms and conditions may vary from trust to trust. Each of the different grades has a scale of pay points, so while a physio is on a certain grade their pay will rise each year until they reach the top pay point of the scale. These increment rises are in addition to the national pay rise that is set each year.

The basic grade is what newly qualified graduates will start on and they will stay on this grade at least until they have completed their two-year rotations. Once these are completed the majority of physios will successfully secure a post at senior II grade, partially because of the demand for senior I and II grades in the health service.

Most experienced physios are on a senior I grade and may or may not have management responsibility, while the superintendent grades tend to be at management level. However, physios regarded as 'clinical specialists' in a particular field are being regraded to the superintendent grade more frequently these days.

The grades are as shown in the box and the figures show the bottom and top of each pay scale (for April 2002 to March 2003).

| | 1st grade 1.4.02 £ | 2nd grade* 1.4.02 £ | 3rd grade 1.4.02 £ | 4th grade 1.4.02 £ | 5th grade 1.4.02 £ | 6th grade 1.4.02 £ | 7th grade 1.4.02 £ |
|---|---|---|---|---|---|---|---|
| Physiotherapist | 17,115 | 17,745 | 18,375 | 19,155 | | | |
| Senior II | 18,375 | 19,155 | 20,045 | 20,935 | 21,825 | 22,875 | 23,405 |
| Senior I | 21,825 | 22,875 | 23,930 | 24,995 | 25,695 | 26,055 | |
| Superintendent IV | 21,825 | 22,875 | 23,930 | 24,995 | 25,695 | 26,055 | |
| Superintendent III | 24,995 | 25,695 | 26,410 | 27,140 | 27,600 | | |
| Superintendent II | 27,140 | 28,060 | 29,010 | 29,990 | | | |
| Superintendent I | 29,990 | 30,970 | 31,990 | 33,020 | | | |
| District II | 33,020 | 34,190 | 35,360 | 36,530 | | | |
| District I | 36,530 | 37,840 | | | | | |
| Student Teacher | 16,495 | 17,115 | 17,745 | 18,375 | | | |
| Teacher | 27,080 | 28,220 | 29,370 | 30,520 | | | |
| Senior Teacher | 29,370 | 30,520 | 31,710 | 32,910 | | | |
| Principal II | 30,520 | 31,710 | 32,910 | 33,940 | | | |
| Principal I | 32,910 | 33,940 | 34,990 | 36,060 | | | |
| Principal 24+ | 36,060 | 37,120 | 38,210 | 39,300 | | | |

* Point for graduate entry with four years' training

The two district grades are very rarely used but, where they are, offer a salary competitive with industry outside of the NHS.

The working week for physiotherapists in the NHS is 36 hours. You may be able to boost your basic salary with other payments, for example on-call duties, when weekend work or bank holiday cover is required.

## Physiotherapy Assistants (Helper Grades)

| Assistant | 1.4.02 | 1.4.02 | 1.4.02 | 1.4.02 | 1.4.02 | 1.4.02 | 1.4.02 | 1.4.02 | 1.4.02 |
|---|---|---|---|---|---|---|---|---|---|
| Age 18 (under supervision) | 10,080 | | | | | | | N/SVQ Level II | N/SVQ Level III |
| 19+ | | 10,450 | 10,740 | 11,070 | 11,400 | 11,740 | 12,110 | 12,480 | 12,850 |

Physiotherapy assistants are not as well paid as qualified physiotherapists because they are not required to undertake the same level of training. Even so, it is acknowledged that assistants are poorly paid and there has been a great deal of work undertaken by the Chartered Society of Physiotherapy, which assistants can join, to increase their pay and improve their terms and conditions.

## Part-time Hourly Rates

| Increments: | 1.4.02 | 1.4.02 | 1.4.02 | 1.4.02 | 1.4.02 | 1.4.02 | 1.4.02 |
|---|---|---|---|---|---|---|---|
| Physio | 9.12 | 9.45* | 9.79 | 10.20 | | | |
| Senior II | 9.79 | 10.20 | 10.68 | 11.15 | 11.63 | 12.18 | 12.47 |
| Senior I | 11.63 | 12.18 | 12.75 | 13.31 | 13.69 | 13.88 | |

* Point for graduate entry with four years' training

Part-time staff are paid pro rata to the appropriate full-time salary scale (including London Weighting where applicable).

There are two main grades for assistants or technical instructors (TIs) and two further TI grades (TI I and TI II), which are rarely used. The pay awards for these grades are as shown in the box (for April 2002 to March 2003).

## Technical Instructor Grade I, Grade II and Grade III

| | 1.4.02 | 1.4.02 | 1.4.02 | 1.4.02 | 1.4.02 |
|---|---|---|---|---|---|
| Grade III | 12,310 | 12,680 | 13,050 | 13,420 | 13,790 |
| Grade II | 14,170 | 14,740 | 15,330 | 15,920 | 16,520 |
| Grade I | 16,640 | 17,500 | 18,360 | 19,230 | 20,100 |

Although a physiotherapy career in the NHS is unlikely to be a highly paid job, there appears to be an increasing recognition that if the NHS is to retain its dedicated workforce it must improve salary levels more in line with the commercial sector. The last two years have seen above-inflation pay rises and the introduction of more family-friendly policies, which will make it easier for people with caring responsibilities to further their careers. This is good news for the thousands of healthcare staff who make up the health service workforce.

# OUTSIDE THE NHS

Private practice can be a more lucrative matter. There are approximately 10,000 physiotherapists working in the independent sector, which encompasses private practitioners, independent hospitals, charities and the voluntary sector, sports clubs and the Ministry of Defence.

Prices for private practice consultations vary according to whether somebody is a sole practitioner or whether they work as part of a larger clinic, and their level of expertise. If a sole practitioner or if employing other staff, the physio will need to organise their own tax and national insurance and cover their own sick leave and holidays.

Independent hospitals have their own pay scales for staff and these are generally marginally higher than NHS pay scales, but not always. Individuals should always check on the salary structure with prospective employers before accepting an offer of employment.

In other areas of the independent sector, such as Premiership or First Division football clubs, a senior I grade may earn anything from £22,000 to £40,000 plus bonuses for wins and cup runs. There may be other perks thrown into the package, such as cars. But there is no 36-hour week for these physios. They are likely to be working six days a week, with long hours, and often a considerable amount of travelling away from home. It may be lucrative, but a high-class sports club will want its pound of flesh from its physio! Physiotherapists who win contracts or are employed by sports clubs are often keen players of the sport themselves, which helps them to cope with the level of dedication expected.

Those who find jobs within the Ministry of Defence as civilian physiotherapists are on the same pay scales and enjoy the same conditions as those in the NHS. There are some physios who are actually members of the armed forces and will be paid according to their rank. There are also physios working in the police force and prison service, who may be self-employed or employed by either of these services.

Physiotherapists working in industry or the occupational health sector can earn good salaries, depending on their employer. Major organisations such as Marks and Spencer and the Royal Mail are just two examples of where physios can work, although this is definitely a growing sector as employers recognise the benefits of on-site healthcare for their workers in minimising disruption and reducing sick leave. (More information about working in industry can be found in Chapter 11, Working in occupational health.)

# Chapter 9
# WORKING IN AN ACUTE HOSPITAL

Physiotherapy offers a range of career opportunities in an acute hospital. Specialist areas of work include orthopaedics, rheumatology, neurology, respiratory care, paediatrics, obstetrics and gynaecology and care of the elderly. Hospitals tend to be extremely busy places and if a hectic lifestyle is not something you enjoy this is probably not the area for you. Although you will still be expected to fulfil all of the routine duties that form part of being a physiotherapist, if you work in a hospital you will never be quite sure just what you are going to encounter each day you go to work.

## CASE STUDY

Mariana works as a physiotherapist in orthopaedics. Some of her time is spent with patients on wards, while the rest is taken up with rehabilitation in the hospital gym. She says: 'My patients are referred from their GP, from consultants within the hospital, or from accident and emergency. Some outpatients have broken legs or stiff joints, while others have had a cartilage operation. The routine is the same as for any other patient. I see them, work out a treatment plan, and see them as many times as they need me to. This can vary between one appointment and several months' worth of appointments. Some are seen in groups, and some are treated one to one. The type of treatment varies, but it can include exercising in the gym, manual therapy and treatment with ultrasound. The inpatients tend to have had hip replacements, knee joint replacements and also spinal operations. The joke they all have is referring to physiotherapists as 'physio-terrorists'. They often dread our visits, because even though they know the exercises we give them will be of benefit, we have to get them up and moving and they are sometimes scared about this. We usually start off with some simple exercises on the ward before moving on to anything more complex. We have to help them get back to an acceptable degree of mobility before they can be discharged from hospital.'

One area that has benefited enormously from physiotherapy input is women's health. Many women suffer from incontinence or back pain following childbirth, and the work of physiotherapists can control this to a large extent.

**CASE STUDY**

Alison runs both ante- and post-natal classes for women, helping them to prepare themselves for childbirth and then to cope with what comes afterwards. She says: 'The classes are offered to all women who have babies at the hospital. Pregnancy puts a huge strain on the body of a woman, and it is only natural that they should want to return to full fitness and be able to perform at the level they did before they had a baby. Each woman is invited to attend a class once a week, and we do exercises to help flatten the tummy and tone up the pelvic floor muscles which have taken the strain of the baby for nine months. The classes also provide a forum for the women to discuss any problems they may be having, both with professionals and with one another, so it forms a support network in that sense. Usually, after ten weeks, the women are sufficiently back into condition to start attending a regular gym in the community, but if there are any problems we have picked up on, then obviously they continue here for longer. It's very satisfying to help people get back into shape and to play a role in educating them how to avoid things such as a bad back by using the correct techniques for picking up their babies.'

# EXTENDED SCOPE PRACTITIONERS

The role of the physiotherapist has developed hugely in recent years, and one of the latest developments in acute hospitals has been the creation of the extended scope practitioner (ESP). These are physiotherapists whose role falls outside the traditional scope of physiotherapy (manual therapy, electrotherapy and exercise and movement). Besides being able to offer manual therapy such as massage and exercise, ESPs can request X-rays, scans, and generally take on responsibility for assessment, diagnosis and management of patients, which may or may not include making referrals to other specialists and listing patients for surgery. This is obviously only possible where physios have in-depth knowledge, which is crucial for patients with conditions involving orthopaedics, respiratory care and neurology.

**CASE STUDY**

Paul is an ESP working in orthopaedics. He says: 'ESPs have shown themselves to be particularly useful in reducing orthopaedic waiting lists. Instead of patients waiting for months to see a consultant, they can see an ESP as a point of first contact. Often it transpires that they do not need to see an orthopaedic consultant, but can be treated by us. This has had a huge effect on shortening the waiting times for those patients who really do need to have a surgical intervention. Although we are working to strict guidelines, I love the extra freedom the role gives me, and patients certainly seem highly satisfied.'

Because of the nature of the work, it is recommended that ESPs have at least five years' broad experience following qualification, at least three years' experience in relevant specialist areas, and have completed an accredited advanced assessment, diagnostic and treatment course.

# MANAGEMENT VERSUS A CLINICAL ROUTE

One option that can be pursued from an early stage in physiotherapy in hospitals is a management route rather than a clinical route. This would move the physio away from a hands-on role with patients to managing staff and budgets, being involved in strategic planning and liaison with other managers on operational and policy issues. The manager is usually the interface between higher authorities in the hospital and the physiotherapy team. One manager describes this as being 'almost like a sales person – you have to go out and gather information and bring it back to your team and sell it to them and to other directorates as well'. Good communication and people skills, organisation and prioritisation skills will be important for any physiotherapist, but particularly for a manager.

Physios who are managers may not just be managing fellow physiotherapists, but may be in charge of a multidisciplinary team of other professions allied to medicine (PAMs), including, for example, speech and language and occupational therapists and chiropodists, or possibly nurses.

There is a CSP occupational interest group for physio managers, called the Association of Chartered Physiotherapists in Management. Contact details can be found at the back of the book.

# Chapter 10
# WORKING IN THE COMMUNITY

For many years community physiotherapy was seen as the poor relation of other, more glamorous areas of the profession. However, recent changes in the health service have seen a rapid expansion of the service and there are now many more opportunities for team-working and specialised roles.

## COMMUNITY CARE

The emphasis on care in the community means that many patients who would formerly have been in hospital now receive treatment in, or close to, their own homes. The wide support network that has developed as a result of this means that patients are now discharged from hospital sooner than they would have been before, receiving health and social care in the community setting. The nature of the work means that a community physiotherapist needs to have a good grasp of the sociological, environmental and economic factors that influence people's lives. They need to be open-minded and able to adapt their work to the conditions in which they find themselves. Community physios often find themselves working alone for a large part of the day, so a good deal of self-sufficiency and problem-solving skills are also required.

### CASE STUDY

Joan works as part of a Primary Care Group, which includes doctors and community nurses. Together with a nurse she devised a rehabilitation programme for patients who had chronic pulmonary disease. She says: 'Some of our patients could barely get out of their homes because they became so breathless. As well as being frustrating for them because they could not do any of the tasks they needed to, it is also very isolating and can lead to other problems such as depression. We devised a ten-week programme of education and rehabilitation to dispel the myths about it being best for them to do as little as possible, and to help them to build up endurance. The group met three times per week in the clinic and we offered a programme of gentle exercise and support. By the end of the ten weeks every person had increased their stamina and was feeling more positive about life, which was a wonderful achievement for both them and us.'

Although much of the work is general, the larger numbers of patients being treated in this setting means that there is more scope than ever before for specialism. Many towns and cities now have specialist teams providing care in the areas of learning disabilities, neurology (stroke rehabilitation), respiratory care, care of the elderly, mental health and paediatrics.

# PAEDIATRICS

In paediatrics physiotherapists have the opportunity to work in both home and school settings, with many going into mainstream schools to work with children who would formerly have been educated in special schools. One result of this is that the physios now have a far bigger teaching role, educating teachers who would not have come into contact with children with special needs under the old system. Physiotherapists are also actively working with schools to help them with ergonomics.

## CASE STUDY

Community physio Joanna says: 'As the problem of repetitive strain injury in adults becomes more widespread, there is no reason to suppose that children are immune to it, so it is important that physios work with teachers to educate them about the need for children to take frequent breaks when they are using computers, and to ensure that the equipment they are using, such as desks and chairs, is ergonomically correct in order to avoid problems in the future. Parents also need to be aware of this when their children are using computers at home. Apart from risks from computers, we teach both teachers and children about the dangers of carrying heavy bags of books to and from school, and encourage the use of backpacks with two straps to distribute the weight more evenly. Many people think of physiotherapy as purely a treatment for existing problems, but one of the joys of the profession is being in a position to prevent injuries occurring in the first place, which is why I enjoy working in schools so much.'

# LEARNING DISABILITIES

**CASE STUDY**

Neil works primarily with young adults with learning disabilities and is part of a community learning disabilities team. He works in social services day centres and residential centres, using a combination of rebound therapy (using a trampoline), hydrotherapy, gymnastics, basic fitness and ball sports such as tennis and squash. He said: 'We use mainly rebound therapy and I have no doubts of the benefits it brings. There is sheer enjoyment on the faces of patients and it is also very effective for toning up muscles and reducing muscle contracture. Hydrotherapy is also very popular. At the moment, rebound therapy and hydrotherapy are the two most requested therapies because the clients have such fun. This is important because, unlike other clients who will usually persevere with treatment because you explain the benefits to them, people with learning disabilities need to enjoy their therapy sessions for their own sake. Communicating requires different skills, especially if the clients have severe disabilities and can't communicate through speech. Gymnastics is another useful therapy. Some people do not like the unpredictability of rebounding and they are happier with a more structured environment. Gymnastics provides this discipline – there is a right and wrong way of doing things and it allows for achievement. One of the negative aspects of working with people with learning disabilities is the lack of understanding among the public and other medical professionals, and also the fact that the work is exhausting and very demanding. However, it can be hugely rewarding and enjoyable, both for the therapist and the clients. I wouldn't do anything else.'

# ADAPTING TO THE WORKING ENVIRONMENT

One of the differences between working in the community compared with working in a hospital setting is the need to adapt to your working environment, including the wide range of people you will find in it. It is possible that you will have more interaction with your patient's carers and it is important to make contact at the earliest opportunity and to explain and agree on the carer's role in the care plan. It goes without saying that the physiotherapist should always be polite and courteous to carers and other people in the patient's home. Meetings, visits and treatment sessions should be arranged to be convenient for the carer as well as the patient.

**CASE STUDY**

Community physiotherapists are known for their resourcefulness. Jane is part of a community physiotherapy team, but works across all patient groups and in all settings. She says: 'One of the best things about my work is the broad range of cases I see, and the many areas in which I work. One client may require treatment in the home, but someone else may need it at college, the shops, the park or even on the bus.' Jane tailors her work totally to her clients' needs. 'The work on the bus involved a man who had suffered a stroke and wanted to get back to doing the family shopping, for which he needed to use the bus. Our work focused on balance and stepping. We also focused on building endurance to ensure that he could actually get around the shops once he got there.' Although Jane feels that working in diverse settings is an important part of her work, she also emphasises the crucial nature of working in the more traditional setting of the home. 'Working with a client in their home environment is very important as you actually adapt your work to the patient's own surroundings. The types of equipment available in hospitals are often not available, so you tailor your work exactly to the physical circumstances in which the person lives, using all sorts of innovative approaches.' Jane's team includes physiotherapists, occupational therapists, a speech therapist, a psychologist, disability workers and advocates. She says: 'Working as part of a multidisciplinary team is a big plus – together you are so much more than the sum of the individual parts and can help people achieve so much more.'

The Association of Chartered Physiotherapists in the Community (ACPC) is able to provide more detailed information on working in this area (see clinical interest and occupational groups at the back of the book).

# Chapter 11
# WORKING IN OCCUPATIONAL HEALTH

People thinking of going into physiotherapy, but not necessarily wanting to work in a traditional healthcare environment, may be interested in specialising in the field of occupational health physiotherapy.

More and more companies are investing in improved occupational health services for their staff, seeing the benefits of reduced sickness rates and quicker returns to work. A physiotherapist is an increasingly important member of the occupational health team in the private and the public sectors, either as a contractor or as an employee. There are physiotherapists employed in a wide range of different working environments, from the police force, the prison service and the armed forces to huge corporations such as Nissan, Rolls-Royce and British Nuclear Fuels Ltd.

Changes in the way people work is also reflected in changes in the delivery of occupational healthcare. For example, call centres have become a fixture of modern day life, particularly in the banking and insurance industries. Owners of these centres, which have literally hundreds of workers taking customer telephone calls, are now turning to specialist physiotherapists to help maintain the health of their workforce and organise work stations in a more ergonomically friendly way.

Many physiotherapists working in this field are dually trained as ergonomists, which means they are able to look at the person's working space, assessing the set-up and possible risks, as well as delivering conventional physiotherapy treatment.

Occupational health is also likely to be a growing area of employment for physios as the government increasingly turns its attention to getting people back into work and recognises the importance of workplace rehabilitation in this goal. This isn't a new thing, however, just a return of emphasis, as the current chair of the CSP's Association of Chartered

Physiotherapists in Occupational Health (ACPOH), Jacqui Smith, can testify.

**CASE STUDY**

Jacqui Smith started to specialise in occupational health very early on in her career after doing some temporary cover work (locums) in a miners' rehabilitation centre, jointly funded by British Coal and the National Health Service. 'I enjoyed that very much from the point of view of being able to get people back to work. At the end of the day that's what rehabilitation is all about,' says Jacqui.

'Moving on from there, I went back into NHS outpatients work, but became very frustrated by the fact that you would get someone well enough to go back to work, and before you knew it they were back with you again. In many cases it was a work-related problem and because the cause wasn't being addressed the physiotherapy wasn't that effective.'

It was at this stage that she started to read about ergonomics with a view to looking at how musculoskeletal problems could be reduced in the workplace. When Jacqui had the opportunity to work at what was then the Ministry of Labour she grabbed it, and before too long she was running her own employment rehabilitation unit. 'It was very exciting. We had people who were unemployed but with disabilities and we were trying to help them into jobs, and we were also helping people who were employed but not working because of an injury.'

Jacqui says that working in occupational health 'just felt a much more complete job to me. In the NHS you're treating people and improving functions but my criteria for success were the social/psychological aspects of getting people back into the workplace and coping. That gave me a huge buzz, and still does.'

During her time with the Ministry Jacqui saw money being cut from internal budgets and more physios being employed on a contractual basis 'because rehab wasn't being done in-house any more. That went on for many years very successfully. For example, in the Yorkshire region, which we covered, there were 30 physiotherapy contracts alone.' At the same time, having reached a senior position in the region, she was able to go out to employers and advise them on improving their work situations, ergonomic set-ups, furniture specifications and so on.

The circle has turned again, as rehabilitation has become a focus for the government with the launch of a new occupational health strategy in the year 2000.

Jacqui's work emphasis started to shift when she found herself being involved with other types of work, such as acting as an expert witness for legal cases. 'In 1989 I was asked by a friend to comment on a work-related injury case, just casually, but ended up acting as an expert witness, and have done over 1000 cases since then. Outside of the work I was already doing it was taking up more of my time. I was also being approached by employers I had known in the past to do ergonomics assessments, and I gradually had more opportunities to do work other than that which I was doing with the Ministry.'

After completing a Masters in Ergonomics a few years later, Jacqui took the plunge and decided to set up her own occupational health and ergonomics consultancy with a colleague. 'We now have occupational health contracts with local authorities and the employment service; doing the job I used to do! I still do a lot of expert witness work on liability and employment-related issues, functional assessment, advice on compliance with the Disability Discrimination Act, risk audit and training.'

One of the possible disadvantages of working in this field is the potential for professional isolation. 'I would never say go straight into the field but build up some experience first,' says Jacqui. 'It is very important to hone your general physiotherapy skills because once you're in occupational health you will often be working alone or as a lone physio within a multidisciplinary team, so professionally that's quite isolating.' This is why Jacqui believes that groups such as ACPOH provide an important support network. 'I am also a member of the Ergonomics Society and I feel that organisations like these give you a point of contact and networking opportunity. For example, if you are faced with a particular problem at work, you don't want to reinvent the wheel, so you can ask colleagues.' She also thinks it is important for newcomers in occupational health to join groups like ACPOH because of the differences from working in standard physiotherapy and for CPD purposes.

So what are her tips for people thinking of going into this area of physiotherapy practice? 'It will appeal to the sort of person who is interested in the big picture. A lot of physiotherapists are very focused on the patient, which is absolutely right, but in occupational health you need to be confident enough to negotiate with people who are not within your own profession to make changes. It also helps to have an interest in the applied side of science, not just the clinical issues. It may also be attractive to people interested in psychology because there are a lot of psycho/social issues in occupational health.'

Jacqui concludes: 'What is vital is that physios get into the workplace and look at what's going on and lobby and communicate with the people who make the decisions to make changes. Sometimes it takes a while, but it's worth it.'

For further information about the Association of Chartered Physiotherapists in Occupational Health turn to the back of the book.

# Chapter 12
# WORKING IN THE INDEPENDENT SECTOR

There are three main sections where physiotherapists work within the independent sector – private practice, independent hospitals and charities.

Working in private practice is generally acknowledged to be a more lucrative area than the NHS, but as the second case study in this chapter clearly shows, this is often related to the fact that the hours worked are longer than in the public sector. Charities such as Scope or The Stroke Association employ physiotherapists and provide a way for specialists to apply their knowledge with a particular client group outside the NHS.

Physiotherapists working in the independent sector are bound by exactly the same code of conduct and core standards as those working in the NHS. However, they may have other factors to consider such as the benefits and disadvantages of working as a sole practitioner, which some can find very lonely, or the difficulties of maintaining continued professional development.

When thinking about working in private practice as opposed to the NHS it is worth looking at the pros and cons of both. The following list is not exhaustive but gives a comparison of the principal issues involved:

## NHS

1. Known and guaranteed income
2. National insurance and income tax deducted from pay
3. Corporate pension scheme (optional if working 18–36 hours per week)
4. Paid holiday
5. Paid sick leave and maternity leave (depending on length of service)

6. Uniform provided or allowance paid
7. Regular contact with colleagues (although increasingly, in areas such as community work, NHS physios may be working in more isolated conditions)
8. Set hours of work plus emergency duties
9. Equipment provided and serviced
10. Further professional training may be funded
11. NHS responsible for insurance cover as an employee
12. Partial responsibility for administration.

# PRIVATE PRACTICE

1. Variable and uncertain income, but potential to earn more than in the NHS
2. Organise payment of own NI contributions; pay tax on profits at year-end
3. Fully fund your own pension
4. Unpaid holidays; must also arrange and pay for locum cover
5. Unpaid sick leave and maternity leave; must insure for loss of earnings and make arrangements for the transfer of patients
6. Provide uniforms at own expense
7. Sole practitioners can feel isolated; contact with colleagues varies and is in your own time and at your own expense
8. Variable hours (often unsocial) according to workload, but greater flexibility than NHS counterparts
9. Buy and service own equipment
10. Training at own expense and involving potential loss of earnings
11. Responsible for own professional insurance cover (however, if member of the Chartered Society of Physiotherapy, this is included in the price of full membership)
12. May be wholly responsible for administration.

**CASE STUDY**

Sammy received some excellent careers advice at the age of 14 and consequently spent time with physiotherapists before moving on to physiotherapy training herself. After qualifying in 1988 she started her career in the NHS and then spent six seasons working in professional football (she was the first female physiotherapist for the FA). Sammy went on to complete a full-time MSc in musculoskeletal dysfunction and then worked in France, Israel, Japan and the US. She attended the World Student Games and has headed up the British Medical Team for the Maccabiah games since 1993. Sammy set up in private practice ten years ago, specialising in outpatients and offering home visits and employing five physiotherapists. She has continued professional development through taking a Masters in Physiotherapy and is now doing an MBA as well as teaching aerobics and pilates.

Before taking the leap into private practice completely, many physiotherapists choose to maintain a part-time post in the NHS in combination with some private work. This might allow the practitioner to build up a client base, expand their skills in their chosen field and potentially earn more money than they would solely in a health service position.

There are two organisations for chartered physiotherapists working in the independent sector: the Organisation of Chartered Physiotherapists in Private Practice (OCPPP) and the Association of Chartered Physiotherapists in Independent Hospitals and Charities (ACPIHC). Both can offer advice and support for their members on the types of issues identified above and provide a networking group for peers. Contacts for both of these organisations can be found in the clinical interest and occupational groups listing at the back of the book.

## CASE STUDY

Chris O'Donoghue has spent the last 20 years working in private practice after spending the first 23 years of her physiotherapy career in the NHS. After graduating in 1958 Chris worked in a hospital outpatients department. She developed her musculoskeletal expertise and became a manipulation specialist, joining the Manipulation Association of Chartered Physiotherapists (MACP). She then did an MPhil and was involved in research for many years. Although she was still working in clinical practice she became involved in a multi-centred trial on sciatica. 'At the end of doing the trial I wasn't quite sure where I was going career-wise, and it was either a choice of going into teaching or being a superintendent somewhere. As I really enjoy the hands-on aspect of physiotherapy the most, neither of those options was very attractive as far as I was concerned.'

Her dilemma was answered when some orthopaedic surgeons who knew of her work in the NHS approached her. She decided to rent a room in private orthopaedic consulting rooms near where she lived and set up her practice. 'I got to know the GPs and the whole thing went from there,' she says.

Chris moved to her own practice after six years, giving her more space and the foundation on which to grow her business. After the move she continued to work on her own for a while, re-establishing the business. Now she employs seven other physiotherapists, all with specialist manipulation skills and most of whom have completed further postgraduate qualifications. The clinic even takes postgraduate students who are honing their manipulation skills, which introduces a teaching element for Chris's staff that they enjoy.

Chris advises physiotherapists thinking of setting up on their own to recognise that when you work in private practice the general economy has a knock-on effect. For example, the 'bust' period of the late 1980s meant that patients with private insurance were losing their jobs and resulted in a downturn in her business. But at the end of this period the GPs in the area went into a fundholding consortium and, says Chris, 'I was able to use my contacts and secure a contract which gradually formed around 50 per cent of my work.' Now that GP fundholding has been abolished Chris is working with the local primary care group (PCG), which brings together local medics in a similar way and her practice has a contract to service patients under the new PCG arrangements.

'If you're going into private practice then it's very important to have really good manual skills,' says Chris. Her clinic's caseload primarily covers backs, necks, sports injuries and some women's health conditions.

Running a busy practice has benefits for Chris and her team. They don't suffer from the professional isolation that sole practitioners might and 'we have a really good in-house CPD programme,' she says. 'We do keep ourselves very much in touch and one or other of us is on a course almost every weekend.'

As for offering advice to people interested in pursuing a physiotherapy career in the independent sector, Chris says the main thing is establishing your reputation. 'You have to get yourself known, by GPs and by a local client base. Once you've got a patient you've treated successfully, they will come back to you. You become part of a community, but it takes time to establish that situation – and nobody can do that quickly.' She also believes that private practitioners should have specialist skills. 'If you're going into private practice, patients don't expect a generalist set-up,' she says.

Chris has always off-loaded the administrative side of the business to her husband. 'One of the things I didn't want to do when I started in private practice was handle the paperwork. I felt I was hands-on and that's what I wanted to continue doing. We have other administrative staff who have also taken a lot of those tasks on board.' Even for the sole practitioner Chris feels it is worthwhile employing or paying somebody to deal with the administrative side.

Chris believes that the future of physiotherapy in the independent sector lies firmly in the delivery of primary care services. And as for the earning potential, she concludes: 'We earn more money than working in the National Health Service but you work much harder for it. The illusion that you earn more in private practice is wrong because the hours aren't comparable. My clinic is open until 10pm one night a week, we routinely work till 8pm and we're often open on Saturdays. The rewards are commensurate with the time that you put in.'

# Chapter 13
# CONTINUING IN EDUCATION/RESEARCH

Completing a physiotherapy degree doesn't automatically lead into clinical practice. Many physiotherapy researchers or tutors follow up their undergraduate degrees with postgraduate qualifications and start to make their mark in the academic world. Others combine their teaching or research work with some clinical work as they feel it is important to keep abreast of clinical developments and want to 'keep their hand in'.

Getting research done is often dependent on who will pay for it, so the availability of funding is frequently a determining factor in how these physios configure their working lives. The research base for physiotherapy is still relatively low, but this is changing, and more money is becoming available from a number of different sources to look at both traditional physiotherapy interventions and new professional developments. It is also a potentially exciting area because the fields in which physiotherapists work are very diverse and so the subject matter for both research and teaching is very varied. Physios in education and/or research write academic papers and submit them to academic publications to share advances with their colleagues. There are also opportunities to present these papers to conferences in the UK and around the world.

While there is a core curriculum for all physiotherapy degrees in the UK, which is approved jointly by the Chartered Society of Physiotherapy and the Council for Professions Supplementary to Medicine, the scope within it is actually quite broad. Many specialist physios are attracted into a teaching role and are able to share their expertise, either as a full-time tutor or by delivering lectures on an occasional basis.

**CASE STUDY**

Paul was originally a patient in a physiotherapy department at the age of 16 after surgery on his hand:'I saw that physios were helping people in a real sense and this could be seen in most of the patients on a daily basis. It also looked like good fun. I had thought of going into lab work but I liked the idea of treating patients and having the real tangible evidence that I was making a difference to them, getting them better, or at least as good as they could be, so I went straight into physiotherapy from sixth form at 18.'

After qualifying Paul worked as a junior member of physiotherapy staff, putting the learning into practice, and then he went to work abroad. On returning to the UK he worked in the NHS in a number of roles where an interest in pain evolved. Paul trained in acupuncture and worked in his local pain clinic, performing acupuncture and offering other pain relief techniques. At this time he was also studying for additional qualifications in health studies and management.

Paul developed a teaching role locally and it was his preference for this rather than management that made him apply for a lecturer's post at Manchester School of Physiotherapy. However, after about two years he wanted to get back to seeing patients and doing research and he developed collaborative research projects with the Manchester and Salford Pain Centre studying the psychophysiology of muscle responses in people with chronic pain. This opened his eyes to how complex pain really was and Paul went on to do an MSc in this area.

He found it increasingly hard to juggle research work and teaching so he moved to the University of Manchester and had a part-time contract with the Manchester and Salford Pain Centre to see patients. This involved working in an interdisciplinary pain programme where a team of physiotherapists, psychologists, nurses and medical specialists collaborated on the management of pain. He completed his PhD during this time, wrote about 20 research papers, contributed to five textbooks on pain and gave lectures all over the world. After six years he moved on to develop his own unit where he could continue his research and clinical interests.

Paul was appointed as the first consultant physiotherapist in the UK at the University of Leicester in the Leicester Warwick Medical School where he is also Senior Lecturer in Pain Management and Rehabilitation. As well as researching into pain and the rehabilitation of people in pain, Paul has a teaching role on the MSc in Pain Management and supervises people doing their higher degrees (PhDs) in the department. In addition he has a clinical commitment in the local hospitals.

Paul says, 'Be sure you want to be a physiotherapist. If you only want a degree – do something else. The training involves not only stiff academic work but also the practical input *and* learning how to deal with vulnerable people, often in tragic situations. It is no picnic. Having said that, the potential to have a broad and fulfilling career is great, and if you don't have such a career then you have not explored the profession fully.'

**CASE STUDY**

Claire had always had an interest in science-related subjects, but wanted a career where she worked closely with people. Work experience during high school demonstrated the wonderful rapport that physios were able to develop with their patients due to the relatively long treatment sessions, and also demonstrated the difference physios made to people's levels of pain and function and the improvement they were able to assist people gain in their quality of life. She qualified in 1990 from the University of Queensland in Brisbane, Australia, at the age of 20.

After graduation Claire worked in a major teaching hospital at home for one year and then travelled for two years working in Canada and in the UK, doing locum work at many major teaching hospitals in London and elsewhere. In 1994 she returned to Brisbane to complete a Masters of Physiotherapy Studies at the University of Queensland, which was a clinically oriented course with high levels of anatomy, physiology and pathology involved.

Claire returned to the UK in 1995 and was employed as an associate at a private practice in south-west London, where she still works. She chose to work in this environment as it provided her with an opportunity to work alongside other manual therapists with postgraduate qualifications and many years of experience and expertise.

Through her work she has developed her career so that, as well as working as a private practitioner, she is also involved in postgraduate teaching as a lecturer and clinical tutor. Claire is also a member and Communications Officer of the MACP (Manipulation Association of Chartered Physiotherapists) executive, working to promote the need for specialisation to junior physiotherapists.

Claire says, 'It is a wonderfully rewarding career, although the amount of work involved both in achieving a degree and developing postgraduate experience is not always reflected in the remuneration received.'

# Chapter 14
# WORKING OVERSEAS

Physiotherapy is a skill in very high demand overseas, with CSP members based in major English-speaking countries such as Australia, Canada and New Zealand, with Australia being the most popular.

There are opportunities to work abroad both as a student, by undertaking an overseas elective (usually of up to three months) and as a qualified physiotherapist. However, the times when you only needed to turn up with your qualifications and a clean uniform are long gone, and a lot of research and planning has to go into making sure your overseas experience is a profitable one, both for you and for your chosen country.

Many physiotherapy students want to work abroad as soon as they are qualified. In some cases this can work out extremely well. However, the CSP urges newly qualified physiotherapists to undertake a period of two years' rotation in the UK, in order to consolidate their university learning and to ensure that when they return to the UK they don't have to start on the bottom rung of the ladder. Some countries are now insisting on this before they will take UK-qualified physiotherapists. Some, such as the US, Canada, Australia and South Africa, also ask you to sit an examination.

The CSP's international affairs adviser in the department of Professional Affairs (PA) has a wide range of information about the registration procedures and working practices of many countries, and you are advised to call her if you are thinking about this option. She will also be able to give you contact details for the professional body/registering body of the country in which you are interested and advise you on the issue of professional liability insurance. Contact the PA department on 020 7306 6633.

When you first start to think about working abroad you will need to consider whether you want to undertake work in a developed country or as a volunteer in a developing area. *Frontline* sometimes carries advertisements for overseas jobs, as do other health magazines and national newspapers such as the *Guardian*. If you take the voluntary option there are many agencies, such as VSO, that offer you the opportunity to share skills with less developed countries. If you decide on the voluntary route, you are advised to gain some experience in paediatrics before you go and to take some reference books with you.

Wherever you decide to go you must negotiate salaries and working conditions before you leave the UK. Scrutinise the contract before you leave and make sure that it is acceptable to you. Working abroad is an exciting opportunity to broaden your horizons, both professional and personal, and physiotherapists are lucky in that their skills are very much in demand.

**CASE STUDY**

Jane volunteered to go to India to work on a project to rehabilitate Tibetan victims of torture. She says: 'Although the work was often very stressful and the year I spent abroad was not a career move, the experiences I had there certainly led me to discover many things about myself that I would never have learnt had I remained in England. As the only physiotherapist at the refugee centre I also learnt to work in a very independent manner. There was no one else for me to rely on and the doctors often had very little understanding of physiotherapy. Many of the people I worked with had psychosomatic as well as physical pain – the result of hours spent suspended with their arms tied behind their backs, or having been poked with the butt ends of rifles. I used relaxation techniques and counselling to help relieve the psychosomatic pain, and a combination of massage, stretching and manipulation for the physical conditions. I worked with children and adults of all ages who had been through the most appalling experiences. Many of them had developed such severe frostbite after escaping from Tibet over the Himalayas that they had had to have feet or legs amputated, so I had to teach them how to walk properly with their artificial limbs to avoid developing back problems. The women also had to be educated into not wearing high heels, as their prosthetic legs could not tolerate it. The whole experience was one I will cherish forever and I hope that in a small way I have managed to improve the lives of those people I treated.'

If you want to contact overseas physiotherapy bodies directly rather than going through the CSP, consult the following:

- The American Physical Therapy Association, 1111 North Fairfax Street, Alexandria, Virginia 22314, USA. Tel: 00 1 703 684 2782 ext 3143. Fax: 00 1 703 684 7343. Website: www.apta.org.
- The Australian Physiotherapy Association, PO Box 6465, Melbourne, Victoria 3004, Australia. (Postal address.) Level 3, 201 Fitzroy Street,

St Kilda, Melbourne 3182. (Street address.) Tel: 00 61 3 9534 9400. Website: www.physiotherapy.asn.au.

■ The Canadian Physiotherapy Association, 2345 Yonge Street, Suite 410, Toronto, Ontario M4P 4E5, Canada. Tel: 00 1 416 932 1888. Fax: 00 1 416 932 9708. Email: information@physiotherapy.ca. Website: www.physiotherapy.ca.

■ The New Zealand Society of Physiotherapists, PO Box 27386, Wellington, New Zealand. Tel: 00 64 4 801 6500. Website: www.physiotherapy.org.nz.

■ The South African Society of Physiotherapy, PO Box 92125, Norwood 2117, Johannesburg, South Africa. Tel: 00 27 11 485 1467. Website: www.physiotherapy.org.za.

# Chapter 15
# RETURNING TO THE PROFESSION

There is a serious shortage of physiotherapists to meet the growing demand both within and outside the NHS. There is also a pool of qualified physiotherapists who left the profession for family, social or education reasons and who are no longer practising.

Once you leave work for a length of time, it is normal to feel a lack of confidence about returning. You may feel that you have lost your skills and knowledge, and that the profession has developed without you and you are unaware of the latest treatments and research. The CSP runs annual refresher courses for members who have taken a career break. Details of these are available from the Society. There are also other, weekend courses, often advertised in *Frontline*.

However, there are not enough of these courses, and the CSP has campaigned strongly for managers within the health service to support physiotherapists who wish to return to work by providing flexible reorientation/refresher programmes locally. These could mirror the two-year rotations undertaken by staff physiotherapists, but could be much shorter in duration.

Managers realise that often the only way to recruit to their posts is to adopt more family-friendly policies and to initiate job-sharing or part-time posts. At the same time, if you are a returner, you must be committed to updating and re-orienting. In most cases you should also be prepared to offer a minimum of nine working hours per week in order to maintain clinical competence and continuity of care.

If you are thinking of returning to the profession you should contact the senior therapy manager in the area where you wish to work to find out whether there are any vacancies and if a learning programme could be arranged. The CSP has factsheets containing further advice and information for potential returners.

**CASE STUDY**

When Barbara was at school there wasn't a large career choice for women and physiotherapy was one of the popular options open to her. She left school and did a six-month probation period followed by exams, which would make or break 'wannabe' physiotherapists. Barbara qualified in 1960 and went on to the Royal Liverpool Children's Hospital, working with youngsters who had long-term health problems such as spina bifida and cerebral palsy. She left to get married and have a family of her own. 'I felt sad I didn't continue,' says Barbara 'But they didn't have part-time positions back then, neither did they have childcare options.'

In 1998 Barbara went back into voluntary work at a special needs school involving physiotherapy. From there she moved on to work with the elderly and developed an interest in obstetrics, geriatrics and incontinence and completed further training in the area. Barbara is now a clinical specialist in women's health and a physiotherapy incontinence adviser. She sees patients one day a week and assesses them for consultants. Barbara is also involved in PR, training and regional initiatives. Her work has led to an executive post of a special interest group, the Association of Chartered Physiotherapists in Women's Health. Barbara says, 'You may not make a million, but your training could lead you into many practice opportunities including working abroad. Find your niche, find the type of physiotherapy you enjoy and develop it.'

# NHSE GUIDANCE ON FINANCIAL SUPPORT AVAILABLE TO RETURNERS

The Department of Health has allocated funds to support the return to practice initiative, focused on areas of the country that experience the most challenging recruitment and retention problems. This initiative is aimed at encouraging former healthcare professionals (nurses, midwives, health visitors, allied healthcare professionals and healthcare scientists) to return to the NHS. Workforce confederations will need to work closely with trusts to ensure that the provision of return to practice programmes is closely linked with employment opportunities in the area.

## Free refresher training/return to practice training

All course fees for refresher training required to equip a healthcare professional who is returning after a gap in practice, to refresh and update their skills, knowledge and practice, should be met.

In nursing, midwifery and health visiting this will include attendance on formal return to practice courses required for re-registration and other forms of refresher training tailored to meet individuals' circumstances to enable those with effective registration to refresh their skills after a short gap in practice.

For other health professionals refresher training may encompass attendance on a variety of courses and retraining on the job.

## £1000 income while retraining

Every health professional required to undertake retraining to equip them to return to practice in the NHS will receive at least £1000 (£1500 for midwives) income to support them while they are retraining. The exact amount of support will be determined by whether or not the returner is employed while retraining (see below). The Inland Revenue has now reached the view that the £1000 payment would not be chargeable to income tax when paid to those who are not employed by the NHS while retraining. This is because the payments are not being made 'for acting as, being or becoming an employee'.

For those who are not employed by the NHS while retraining the £1000 payments will be made over the period of the training directly to the individual concerned. Local confederations/NHS employers may at their discretion and in the light of recruitment and retention difficulties supplement this payment to take account of individual financial circumstances, local labour market conditions and/or the length of the training period. Confederations will need to implement a locally agreed mechanism for payment, including how many instalments the support will be paid in.

For those who are employed in the NHS while retraining the £1000 payments should be made to the employer, to subsidise the salary paid during retraining for healthcare professionals not required to undertake a formal retraining programme outside their employment; this sum should subsidise their supernumerary status while they are updating their skills and preparing for a full return to practice.

Confederations should ensure that those retraining while employed are not at any financial disadvantage compared to those who are unemployed and receiving the £1000 payment directly. Confederations and employers are encouraged to offer salary support to returners as good practice, particularly in areas with recruitment and retention difficulties.

## Assistance with childcare

For parents who are not employed while retraining, assistance with childcare costs incurred while attending refresher training and associated clinical placements should be provided up to Working Families Tax Credit levels. Confederations should work with local employers and childcare co-ordinators to help returners access suitable, affordable childcare support, including places in the new NHS nurseries. They should also provide flexible and part-time training options that are sensitive to the circumstances of returners who are parents or have other care responsibilities.

For parents who are employed while retraining, employers and local childcare co-ordinators should help returners access suitable, affordable childcare, including access to the childcare support available through the Working Families Tax Credit, where applicable. They should also provide flexible and part-time training options that are sensitive to the circumstances of returners who are parents or have other care responsibilities.

## Travel, subsistence, books and other individual expenses

Assistance with reasonable travel, subsistence, books and other individual expenses associated with the return process should be provided. Local confederations will wish to set guidance on the amount of reimbursement available for subsistence and books.

# Chapter 16
# PHYSIOTHERAPY ASSISTANTS

There are currently approximately 3500 physiotherapy assistants working within the NHS. No formal training is required to gain employment as an assistant, though managers will look for an interest in healthcare and good communication skills, as well as a commitment to learn.

The majority of assistants work in acute hospital trusts, in outpatient departments and with elderly inpatients. Approximately 600 work in the community. The role of the assistant varies enormously, depending on their competence and their place of work. Broadly speaking they are there to help qualified physiotherapists with the delivery of care to patients. This can vary from providing simple walking aids to undertaking part of the treatment programme that has been decided by the physiotherapist.

Provision of education for physiotherapy assistants is varied, though many are encouraged to study for NVQs/SVQs. The CSP's Charitable Trust also makes awards for assistants wishing to study for accredited/validated programmes, such as BTEC awards, Access courses and Professional Development Programmes. Further information is available from the CSP's Professional Affairs department.

Recent research has shown that almost 10 per cent of physiotherapy assistants would like to become qualified physiotherapists. There are currently two part-time degree programmes aimed specifically at assistants, one at Colchester Institute and one at the University of Southampton.

To be eligible for the course at Colchester Institute you should normally be over 21 years of age, and priority is given to applicants who work as physiotherapy assistants within the Eastern Regional Office. Students study on a part-time basis at the Institute, while continuing their work as a physiotherapy assistant part time. Applications for the programme should be made directly to the Institute and not through UCAS. Further information is available by contacting the Institute at Sheepen Road, Colchester, Essex CO3 3LL. Tel: 01206 518777. Email: info@colch-inst.ac.uk. Website: www.colch-inst.ac.uk.

The course at the University of Southampton is sponsored by the South East Regional Office and therefore is open only to assistants working in this area. Again, students should be over 21 years of age and will study for two days per week at the university while continuing to work as a physiotherapy assistant on a part-time basis. Applications for this programme are also made directly to the university, and anyone who is interested should contact the university at Highfield, Southampton SO17 1BJ. Tel: 023 8059 5000. Email: admissns@soton.ac.uk. Website: www.soton.ac.uk.

The entry requirement for both of these courses is the same as for full-time courses (see the list of university programmes at the back of the book).

The CSP has initiated a programme known as 'Oiling the Gate' to enable applicants without the standard A-level qualifications to gain access on to a tailor-made physiotherapy foundation programme. Successful completion of this course allows students to move on to the full degree course.

# Chapter 17
# THE PROFESSIONAL BODIES

## THE CHARTERED SOCIETY OF PHYSIOTHERAPY

The Chartered Society of Physiotherapy (CSP) is the national body for physiotherapists in the UK and has around 40,000 members. It covers professional and educational matters and is also a trade union, so it has what is called a 'tripartite' function. Most of physiotherapists in the UK belong to the CSP. The figures quoted in this book concerning the areas in which physiotherapists in the UK work are taken from official CSP sources. As a tripartite organisation, the Society has three core service departments – the Education, Professional Affairs and Industrial Relations departments.

## Education department

The Education department validates all the physiotherapy degrees in the UK and works with the universities to ensure that standards are being maintained, that the core curriculum is being covered, and it offers support over issues such as providing enough clinical placements for students. It also has a careers information line (020 7306 6600) for people wanting to enter the profession, and covers postgraduate education and continuing professional development (CPD).

The Education department manages the CSP's Information Resource Centre. This is the national bibliographic information centre for physiotherapy and includes a general information service as well as offering more specialist advice, such as holding a collection of theses and dissertations.

## Professional Affairs department

The Professional Affairs department exists to offer support and guidance primarily to physios and physiotherapy assistants. It covers the legal and ethical framework in which physiotherapists practice, has an integral Clinical Effectiveness Unit and manages the members' clinical interest and occupational group network (see the back of the book for details).

It also oversees the CSP's Rules of Professional Conduct to which all chartered physiotherapists (as well as students) have to adhere. (See pages 66–68 for a copy of the rules.) The CSP often works in tandem with the Health Professions Council (HPC) on disciplinary issues, as the HPC holds the state register for physiotherapists. To work in the National Health Service physios must be state registered and a lapse in registration can be a serious offence.

## Industrial Relations department

The Industrial Relations department covers the trade union aspects of the Society's work. It deals with salaries and employment matters for all members, whether in the NHS, the independent sector or in industry. The CSP is affiliated to the TUC and also holds the staff side secretariat on the General Whitley Council, the body that currently negotiates pay and terms and conditions for physiotherapists and other healthcare professions in the NHS.

Members of the CSP are entitled to receive its two publications, *Frontline* and *Physiotherapy*, a clinical and academic journal. *Frontline* covers the latest developments in the profession, health news and politics, and features many different aspects of physiotherapy practice.

New briefing and information papers are continually released by the CSP on all of the above areas and members can access much of this free of charge. The Society's website is another good source of information and this is regularly updated. Although there are some areas that are protected for member use only there are lots of interesting areas that can be opened up by any Internet user.

Contact with the CSP can be made either through the website or by writing to: Chartered Society of Physiotherapy, 14 Bedford Row, London WC1R 4ED. Tel: 020 7306 6666 (central switchboard). Fax: 020 7306 6611. Website: www.csp.org.uk.

# THE HEALTH PROFESSIONS COUNCIL

The Health Professions Council (HPC) replaces the Council for Professions Supplementary to Medicine (CPSM), which dates back to the 1960s. A UK-wide, independent regulatory body, the HPC will maintain a register of qualified practitioners and will have wider powers to deal effectively with individuals who pose a risk to patients. Tel: 020 7840 9802. Website: www.hpcuk.org.

# PROTECTION OF TITLE

Protection of title is one of the issues that both the CSP and the CPSM are much concerned with and reflects their commitment to protecting people who use physiotherapy services from bogus or unqualified practitioners. At the moment there is no legislation governing who may call themselves a physiotherapist or, a term commonly used internationally, a physical therapist.

Only chartered or state registered physiotherapists are allowed to work within the NHS in the UK. However, in the private sector, anyone can set up as a physiotherapist and the only way of knowing if a physiotherapist is qualified to treat patients and has undertaken an approved course of study is to check that they are chartered or state registered. A chartered physiotherapist will have the letters MCSP (Member of the Chartered Society of Physiotherapy) after their name, while someone who is state registered will follow their name with SRP (State Registered Physiotherapist).

# RULES OF PROFESSIONAL CONDUCT

All healthcare professionals have a code of conduct to which they are expected to adhere. The eight rules are there to protect both physiotherapists and their patients and, if a physio is found to have broken one or more of them, he or she can be disciplined and even struck off. The rules apply to student physiotherapists as well as qualified CSP members. Students found to be in breach of the rules could be dismissed from their course, so it is of the utmost importance that physios acquaint themselves with the rules from the beginning of their training and career.

## Rule I: Scope of practice

Chartered physiotherapists shall only practise to the extent that they have established and maintained their ability to work safely and competently, and shall ensure that they have appropriate professional liability cover for that practice.

## Rule II: Relationships with patients

Chartered physiotherapists shall respect the rights, dignity and individual sensibilities of every patient.

## Rule III: Confidentiality

Chartered physiotherapists shall ensure the confidentiality and security of information acquired in a professional capacity.

## Rule IV: Relationships with professional staff and carers

Chartered physiotherapists shall communicate and co-operate with professional staff and other carers in the interests, and with the consent, of their patient and shall avoid criticism of any of them.

## Rule V: Duty to report

Chartered physiotherapists have a duty to report, to an appropriate authority, circumstances which may put patients or others at risk.

## Rule VI: Advertising

Chartered physiotherapists shall ensure that any advertising in respect of their professional activities is accurate, professionally restrained and conforms to the British Codes of Advertising Practice and Sales Promotion.

## Rule VII: Sales and services of goods

Chartered physiotherapists shall not sell, supply, endorse or promote the sale of services or goods in ways which exploit their professional relationship with their patient.

## Rule VIII: Personal and professional standards

Chartered physiotherapists shall adhere at all times to personal and professional standards, which reflect credit on the profession.

# GLOSSARY

**Clinical placement** All physiotherapy undergraduate students are expected to complete approximately 1000 hours of clinical placements. To do this they will work in a healthcare setting, under the supervision of qualified physiotherapists, to put into practice what they have learnt in the classroom. They will be assessed on these placements and some of their placements will contribute to their final degree classification.

**Continuing Professional Development** Known as CPD for short, this refers to an ongoing process to update and increase knowledge and skills. It is not currently mandatory, but it is implicit within the Rules of Professional Conduct. (See Chapter 17, The professional bodies, for details.)

**Electrotherapy** This covers a range of treatments used by some physiotherapists and includes the use of equipment such as ultrasound and shortwave diathermy machines. It also includes the use of aids such as ice and wax in the treatment of a patient.

**Inpatients** This generally refers to patients in a hospital or other healthcare setting; unlike outpatients, they are resident in the hospital.

**Mobilisation** This broadly refers to the use of a physiotherapist's manual skills in treating a range of conditions to increase a patient's mobility or more specifically the mobility of a joint. Some forms of mobilisation employ highly specialised techniques.

**Multidisciplinary** This often refers to physiotherapists working alongside other professionals in health and social care settings. There are an increasing number of multidisciplinary teams working in the NHS.

**Musculoskeletal** This pertains to the muscles and the skeleton. This is one element of physiotherapy application and some physios develop their skills in this area to become musculoskeletal specialists treating, for example, sports injuries and low back pain.

**Outpatients** This generally refers to departments in a hospital or other healthcare setting where patients attend for assessment and treatment on a day-only basis (ie not requiring an overnight stay).

**Rehabilitation** Rehabilitation is an interactive process between the patient and the physiotherapist. It aims to restore the individual or part to normal or near-normal function.

**Rotations** A period, usually for a minimum of two years, where a newly qualified physiotherapist undertakes blocks of work in different settings/specialties within the NHS to consolidate their undergraduate training.

**Specialism** A specific field of physiotherapy practice.

**Specialist** Refers to a physiotherapist who has specialist knowledge and experience to practise in a certain area. He or she will usually have undertaken extensive additional training and development and sometimes, but not always, additional qualifications.

# CLINICAL INTEREST AND OCCUPATIONAL GROUPS

There are now some 50 groups representing the diverse interests and specialities of physiotherapists via clinical interest and occupational groups. They have to fulfil strict criteria to be approved by the Society and, while there are many that have approved status, there are a number awaiting approval. These are also listed below. The contacts given are for the current membership secretaries at the time of going to press. Please contact the CSP for further information (www.csp.org.uk).

## CLINICAL INTEREST GROUPS

**AACP** Acupuncture Association of Chartered Physiotherapists

Vibeke Dawson, Mere Complementary Practice, Castle Street, Mere, Wiltshire BA12 6JE.

**ACPICR** Association of Chartered Physiotherapists Interested in Cardiac Rehabilitation

Sushma Sanghvi, Physiotherapy Department, Northwick Park Hospital, Watford Road, Harrow, Middlesex HA1 3UJ.

**ACPAT** Association of Chartered Physiotherapists in Animal Therapy

Mrs J Verey, Morland House, Salters Lane, Winchester, Hampshire SO22 5JP.

**ACPC** Association of Chartered Physiotherapists in the Community

Anne Moir, Inverbervie Health Centre, Church Street, Inverbervie, DD10 0RU, Scotland.

**ACPCF** Association of Chartered Physiotherapists in Cystic Fibrosis

Mary Dodd, Bradbury Cystic Fibrosis Unit, Wythenshawe Hospital, Southmoor Rd, Manchester M23 9LT.

**ACPEM** Association of Chartered Physiotherapists in Energy Medicine

Julie Lygo, 3 Burleigh Road, West Bridgeford, Nottingham NG2 6FP.

**ACPIE** Association of Chartered Physiotherapists Interested in Electrotherapy

Sarah Bazin, Physiotherapy Department, Solihull Hospital, Lode Lane, Solihull, West Midlands B91 2JL.

**ACPIM** Association of Chartered Physiotherapists Interested in Massage

Sarah Varman, Malthouse Cottages, Honesty Bottom, Bright Walton, Nr Newbury, Berks RG20 7BD.

**ACPIN** Association of Chartered Physiotherapists in Neurology

Rowena Wright, 27 Oatlands Drive, Harrogate, North Yorkshire HG2 8JT.

**ACPIRT** Association of Chartered Physiotherapists in Reflex Therapy

Alison Stain, 3 Whichcote Avenue, Meriden, Coventry, West Midlands CV7 7LR.

**ACPOM** Association of Chartered Physiotherapists in Orthopaedic Medicine

Ms Lyn Ankcorn, 23 Swarthmore Road, Selly Oak, Birmingham B29 4NQ.

**ACPOPC** Association of Chartered Physiotherapists in Oncology and Palliative Care

Katherine Malhotra, Physiotherapy Department, Royal Marsden Hospital, Fulham Road, London SW3 6JJ.

**ACPPLD** Association of Chartered Physiotherapists for People with Learning Disabilities

Sue Standing, Hawthorn Lodge, Moor Green Hospital, Botley Road, West End, Southampton SO30 3JB.

**ACPRC** Association of Chartered Physiotherapists in Respiratory Care

Alison Gilbert, Department of Physiotherapy, School of Health Science, University of Liverpool, Brownlow Hill, Liverpool L69 3GB.

**ACPSM** Association of Chartered Physiotherapists in Sports Medicine

Christine Wallace, 75 West Street, Grange Villa, Chester le Street, Durham DH2 3LP.

**ACPTR** Association of Chartered Physiotherapists in Therapeutic Riding

Miss Geraldine Walker, The Orchard, Broadlands, Lower Paice Lane, Medstead, Hants GU34 5PX.

**ACPVR** Association of Chartered Physiotherapists in Vestibular Rehabilitation

**ACPWH** Association of Chartered Physiotherapists in Women's Health

Ann Pearson, 1 Mill Ford, Gildersome, Leeds, West Yorkshire LS27 7YQ.

**AGILE** Chartered Physiotherapists Working with Older People

Ms Bhanu Ramaswamy, Physiotherapy Department, Northern General Hospital, Herries Road, Sheffield S5 7AU.

**AOCP** Association of Orthopaedic Chartered Physiotherapists

Ash Shattock, 8 Acre Road, Kingston, Surrey KT2 6EF.

**APCP** Association of Paediatric Chartered Physiotherapists

Christine Shaw, 42 Cammo Grove, Edinburgh EH4 8EX.

**BABTT** British Association of Bobath Trained Therapists

Mrs Rosemary Sudlow, 82 Burnham Road, Leigh-on-Sea, Essex SS9 2JS.

**BACPAR** British Association of Chartered Physiotherapists in Amputee Rehabilitation

Mrs P Unia, Prosthetics Service, Chapel Allerton Hospital, Chapeltown Road, Leeds LS7 4SA.

**BAHT** British Association of Hand Therapists Ltd

Keith Foster 25 Mount View, Billericay, Essex CM11 1HB.

**BBA** British Burns Association

**BBTA** Bobath Tutors

**CPHIV**  Chartered Physiotherapists Interested in HIV

**CPMH**  Chartered Physiotherapists in Mental Healthcare

Clare Leonard, 41 Roman Way, Lechlade, Glos GL7 3BS.

**CPPC**  Chartered Physiotherapists Promoting Continence

**CTACP**  Craniosacral Therapy Association of Chartered Physiotherapists

Cas Boddam-Whitham, Greystones, Rockness Hill, Nailsworth, Glos GL6 0JT.

**HACP**  Hydrotherapy Association of Chartered Physiotherapists

Heather Malling, 40 Cumbeth Close, Crickhowell, Powys NP8 1DX.

**HCPA**  Haemophilia Chartered Physiotherapists Association

**MACP**  Manipulation Association of Chartered Physiotherapists

Mrs Dionne Ryder MSc, Department of Physiotherapy, University of Hertfordshire, College Lane, Hatfield, Herts AL10 9AB.

**MIMDT**  McKenzie Institute Mechanical Diagnosis and Therapy Practioners

Julie Shepherd (Chair) MIMDT, The McKenzie Institute (UK) Trust, Hill Farm Barn, Bruen Road, Milton-under-Wychwood, Oxon OX7 6HB.

**PFH**  Physiotherapy for Hyperventilation

**PPA**  The Physiotherapy Pain Association (for Chartered Physiotherapists)

Peter Gladwell , Physiotherapy Department, Frenchay Hospital, Bristol BS16 1LE.

**RCACP**  Rheumatic Care Association of Chartered Physiotherapists

Susan Hesketh, Physiotherapy Department, Wrightington Hospital, Hall Lane, Wigan WN6 9E.

**SINetwork**  Sensory Integration Network (UK and Ireland)

**SPIUPLC**  National Spinal Injuries Units Physiotherapy Lead Clinicians

# OCCUPATIONAL GROUPS

**ACPIHC** Association of Chartered Physiotherapists in Independent Hospitals and Charities

Tess Thompson, Denton, 63 Fairview Road, Headley Down, Hampshire GU35 8HQ.

**ACPIMM** Association of Chartered Physiotherapists in Military Management

**ACPM** Association of Chartered Physiotherapists in Management

Angela Clayton Turner, 33 Pelham Road, Beckenham, Kent BR3 4SQ.

**ACPOH** Association of Chartered Physiotherapists in Occupational Health and Ergonomics

Jaqui Smith, Smith Denton Associates, c/o The Cottage, Hornsea Road, Atwick, Driffield YO25 8DG.

**AVICP** Association of Visually Impaired Chartered Physiotherapists

**CPE** Chartered Physiotherapists in Education

Ms Fleur Kitsell, School of OT and PT, University of Southampton, Highfield, Southampton SO17 1BJ.

**ESP** Chartered Physiotherapists Working as Extended Scope Practitioners

Cathy Barrett, Physiotherapy Department, St Mary's Hospital, Praed Street, Paddington, London W2 1NR.

**M-LACP** The Medico-Legal Association of Chartered Physiotherapists

Mrs Zena Schofield, 3 Eliot Park, Blackheath, London SE13.

**OCPPP** The Organisation of Chartered Physiotherapists in Private Practice

May Surgeoner, Cedar House, Bell Plantation, Watling Street, Towcester, North Hants NN12 6HN.

**PPIMS** Paediatric Physiotherapists in Management Support

Ms Dawn Sewards, Physiotherapy Manager, Royal Manchester Children's Hospital, Hospital Road, Pendlebury, Manchester M27 4HA.

# DEGREE PROGRAMMES IN THE UK AND THE REPUBLIC OF IRELAND

**Applications to the following courses are made through:**

UCAS, PO Box 28, Cheltenham, Glos GL50 3SF.

## GREAT BRITAIN

### Aberdeen (The Robert Gordon University)

School of Health Sciences, Department of Physiotherapy, The Robert Gordon University, Woolmanhill, Aberdeen AB25 1LD. Contact: Mrs Anne Wallace, Admissions Tutor. Tel: 01224 627146. Website: www.rgu.ac.uk/subj/healthsci.

### Birmingham

School of Health Sciences (Physiotherapy), University of Birmingham, Physiotherapy – Morris House, Edgbaston, Birmingham B15 2TT. Contact: Jacky Conduit, Admissions Tutor. Tel: 0121 627 2020. Website: www.bham.ac.uk.

### Bradford

Division of Physiotherapy, School of Health Studies, University of Bradford, Unity Building, 25 Trinity Road, Bradford, West Yorkshire BD5 0BB. Contact: Judith Hinton, Admissions Tutor. Tel: 01274 236323. Website: www.brad.ac.uk/acad/health.

### Brighton

School of Health Professions, Faculty of Health, University of Brighton, Robert Dodd Building (Eastbourne Campus), 49 Darley Road,

Eastbourne BN20 7UR. Contact: Fiona Jones, Admissions Tutor. Tel: 01273 643660. Website: www.brighton.ac.uk.

## Bristol (University of the West of England)

School of Allied Health Professions, Faculty of Health and Social Care, University of the West of England, Glenside Campus, Blackberry Hill, Stapleton, Bristol BS16 1DD. Contact: The Faculty Admissions Office. Tel: 0117 344 8555. Website: www.uwe.ac.uk.

## Cardiff (University of Wales)

Department of Physiotherapy Education, Ty Dewi Sant, School of Health Care Studies, University of Wales College of Medicine, Heath Park, Cardiff CF14 4XN. Contact: Admissions Tutor. Tel: 029 2074 2267. Website: www.uwcm.ac.uk/hc/index.html.

## Coventry

School of Health and Social Sciences, Coventry University, Priory Street, Coventry CV1 5FB. Contact: Mrs R Gutteridge, Admissions Tutor. Tel: 024 7683 8903. Website: www.coventry.ac.uk.

## Edinburgh (Queen Margaret University College)

Department of Physiotherapy, Queen Margaret University College, Leith Campus, Duke Street, Edinburgh EH6 8HF. Contact: Dr Fiona McMillan, Admissions Tutor. Tel: 0131 317 3666. Website: www.qmced.ac.uk.

## Glasgow

Department of Physiotherapy, Podiatry and Radiography, Glasgow Caledonian University, City Campus, Cowcaddens Road, Glasgow G4 0BA. Contact: Dr Valerie Webster, Programme Organiser. Tel: 0141 331 8116. Website: www.gcal.ac.uk.

# Hertfordshire

Department of Physiotherapy, Faculty of Health and Human Sciences, University of Hertfordshire, Hatfield Campus, College Lane, Hatfield, Hertfordshire AL10 9AB. Contact: Jon Alltree. Tel: 01707 284975. Website: www.herts.ac.uk.

# Huddersfield

School of Human and Health Sciences, University of Huddersfield, Division of Physiotherapy, Ramsden Building, Queensgate, Huddersfield HD1 3DH. Contact: Mrs G Robinson, Admissions Tutor. Tel: 01484 472701. Website: www.hud.ac.uk.

# Keele

Department of Physiotherapy Studies, Mackay Building, Keele University, Keele, Staffordshire ST5 5BG. Contact: Sandy Robertson, Admissions Tutor. Tel: 01782 584196. Website: www.keele.ac.uk/depts/pt/index.html.

# Leeds

School of Health Sciences, Faculty of Health and Environment (Physiotherapy), Leeds Metropolitan University, Calverley Street, Leeds LS1 3HE. Contact: Mark Lewis, Admissions Tutor. Tel: 0113 283 2600 x3304. Website: www.lmu.ac.uk.

# Liverpool

Department of Allied Health Professions, Division of Physiotherapy, University of Liverpool, Thompson Yates Building, The Quadrangle, Brownlow Hill, Liverpool L69 3GB. Contact: The Admissions Secretary. Tel: 0151 794 5712. Website: www.liv.ac.uk.

# London (Brunel University)

Faculty of Life Sciences, Department of Health and Social Care, Brunel University, Lancaster House, Borough Road, Isleworth, Middlesex

TW7 5DU. Contact: Admissions Tutor (Physiotherapy). Tel: 020 8891 0121. Website: www.brunel.ac.uk/depts/health/physio.html.

## London (King's College)

Physiotherapy Division, GKT School of Biomedical Sciences, King's College London, Shepherd's House, Guy's Campus, London SE1 1UL. Contact: Admissions Tutor. Tel: 020 7848 6338. Website: www.kcl.ac.uk/physiotherapy.

## London (St George's Hospital Medical School)

School of Physiotherapy, Faculty of Health and Social Care, St George's Hospital Medical School, 2nd Floor Grosvenor Wing, Cranmer Terrace, London SW17 0RE. Contact: Secretary to School of Physiotherapy. Tel: 020 8725 2274. Website: www.sghms.ac.uk.

## London (University of East London)

Department of Health Sciences, Faculty of Science and Health, University of East London, Romford Road, Stratford, London E15 4LZ. Contact: Barbara Catwell, Admissions Tutor. Tel: 020 8590 7722. Website: www.uel.ac.uk.

## Manchester

School of Physiotherapy, Manchester Royal Infirmary (University of Manchester), Oxford Road, Manchester M13 9WL. Contact: Admissions Tutor. Tel: 0161 276 8709. Website: www.msop.ac.uk.

## Newcastle

Faculty of Health, Social Work and Education, University of Northumbria at Newcastle, Coach Lane Campus, Newcastle upon Tyne NE7 7XA. Contact: Faculty Admissions Office. Tel: 0191 227 3575. Website: www.unn.ac.uk.

## Norwich (University of East Anglia)

School of Occupational Therapy and Physiotherapy, The Queen's Building, University of East Anglia, Norwich NR4 7TJ. Contact: Gill Emanuel on 01603 593063 or Patricia Porritt on 01603 593177. Website: www.uea.ac.uk.

## Nottingham

Division of Physiotherapy Education, Clinical Sciences Building, University of Nottingham, Hucknall Road, Nottingham NG5 1PG. Contact: Admissions Tutor. Tel: 0115 840 4881. Website: www.nottingham.ac.uk.

## Oxford

School of Health Care (Physiotherapy), Oxford Brookes University, Department of Rehabilitation, Dorset House, 58 London Road, Headington, Oxford OX3 7PE. Contact: Physiotherapy Secretary. Tel: 01865 485257. Website: www.brookes.ac.uk.

## Salford

School of Healthcare Professions, University of Salford, Frederick Road Campus, Frederick Road, Salford M6 6PU. Contact: Admissions Tutor. Tel: 0161 295 2280. Website: www.salford.ac.uk.

## Sheffield

School of Health and Social Care, Sheffield Hallam University, Collegiate Crescent Campus, Sheffield S10 2BP. Contact: Admissions Office, 4th Floor Surrey Building, Sheffield Hallam University, Pond Street, Sheffield S1 1WB. Tel: 0114 225 3245. Website: www.shu.ac.uk.

## Southampton

School of Health and Rehabilitation Science, University of Southampton, Highfield, Southampton SO17 1BJ. Contact: Belinda Hatch, General

Enquiries or Mrs Debbie Thackray, Admissions Tutor.
Tel: 023 8059 5260. Website: www.soton.ac.uk/direct/dir104.html.

## Teesside

School of Health and Social Care (Physiotherapy), University of
Teesside, Centuria Building, Borough Road, Middlesborough TS1 3BA.
Contact: Admissions Tutor for BSc programme, Jillian Kent. Tel: 01642
384115. Contact: Admissions Tutor for MSc programme, Brian Houston.
Tel: 01642 384115. Website: www.tees.ac.uk.

# NORTHERN IRELAND

School of Health Sciences – Physiotherapy, Faculty of Social, Health
Sciences and Education, University of Ulster at Jordanstown, Shore
Road, Newtownabbey, Co Antrim, Northern Ireland BT37 0QB.
Contact: Course Director, BSc Hons Physiotherapy. Tel: 028 9036 6096.
Website: www.ulst.ac.uk.

**The following institutions can be approached directly:**

## Colchester

Faculty of Music, Arts and Health (Physiotherapy), Colchester Institute,
Sheepen Road, Colchester, Essex CO3 3LL. Contact: Mrs J Jackson. Tel:
01206 518165. Website: www.colch-inst.ac.uk.

## York

York St John College, Lord Mayor's Walk, York YO31 7EX.
Contact: Course Leader for Physiotherapy. Tel: 01904 716968.
Website: www.yorksj.ac.uk.

# REPUBLIC OF IRELAND

School of Physiotherapy, Mater Misericordiae Hospital, University
College Dublin, Eccles Street, Dublin 7, Republic of Ireland.

Contact: Dr Mary Garrett, Head of Department. Tel: 00 353 1 716 7777. Website: www.ucd.ie.

School of Physiotherapy, Trinity Centre for Health Sciences, St James' Hospital, James's Street, Dublin 8, Republic of Ireland. Contact: Admissions Office, University of Dublin, Trinity College. Tel: 00 353 1 608 2003. Website: www.tcd.ie.

School of Physiotherapy, Royal College of Surgeons in Ireland, 123 St Stephen's Green, Dublin 2, Republic of Ireland. Contact: Professor Marie Guidon. Tel: 00 353 1 402 2397. Website: www.rcsi.ie.